Naked and Exposed

Naked
and
Exposed

Learning to Love Well
Using the Intimacy for Life Method™
in Your Marriage

Dr. Shanon Roberts
First Edition

Naked and Exposed

Learning to Love Well Using the Intimacy for Life Method in Your Marriage

This publication is designed to provide accurate and authoritative information in regard to the subject matter covered. It is sold with the understanding that neither the author nor the publisher is engaged in rendering legal or other professional services. While the publisher and author have used their best efforts in preparing this book, the purpose of this book is to educate and give suggestions. The authors and publisher shall have neither liability nor responsibility to any person or entity with respect to any loss or damage caused or alleged to have been caused directly or indirectly by the information contained in this book.

The stories in this book are based on recurrent themes that have come up in my counseling practice over the years. All these stories are fictitious.

Printed in the United States of America

First Edition

ISBN 979-8-218-25282-3 paperback
ISBN 979-8-218-25283-0 ebook
Library of Congress Control Number: 2023913620

Cover and Interior Design by:
Chris Treccani

Created with the Book to Millions® Method

Included with your purchase of *Naked and Exposed* are several Book Bonuses:
1. Personalized Marital Assessment
2. Digital Resources
3. Training Videos
4. Additional Training and Information

Naked and Exposed will walk you through the Intimacy for Life Method.™ As a seasoned therapist who has worked with countless couples, I know that you can create a relationship full of intimacy, communication, and connection with the one you love.

This book is for couples at all stages and provides:
- A roadmap to help those at the beginning of a relationship chart their path.
- A tool to help couples mired in problems get unstuck and improve things.
- A blueprint to enhance and deepen relationships that are going well.

NakedandExposed.com/Resources

DEDICATION

For my Heavenly Father, the ultimate Parent.
Thank you for your love, care and comfort throughout my life,
my Constant.

CONTENTS

INTRODUCTION

The husband-and-wife relationship is one of the most important relationships God designed. I am witness to its importance both in my personal life and in my work as a therapist.

I was married to a pastor for 30 years and experienced this beautiful bond. Five years ago, I learned firsthand the pain of losing that intimate bond, because it happened to me. Looking back, I can recognize when my marriage began to erode. Once the process started, it proceeded very quickly.

As a Christian woman, wife, mother, and counselor, my sense of shame was heightened. Many Christian couples feel condemned simply because they need *help*. Christian couples don't want to divorce—they want to get back to a close connection. When a downward spiral in my partner's choices prevented us from reaching the next chapter of intimacy and connection, I found myself in an abyss, trying to hold and allow space for hope.

Some people hold this kind of hope for months, years, or even decades. Hope makes us want to move forward. My hope and desire to help my marriage, coupled with my extensive research in my doctoral program, led me to understand the tools both personally and professionally that can move the dial for Christian couples.

The next chapter for Christian couples is not found in an abyss with a glimmer of hope but in moving forward into an intentional place of togetherness. In this place of togetherness, couples can renew the safety and security of their marriage bond.

In my case, sadly, there were personal factors that prevented my husband and I from renewing the safety and security of our relationship, situations that kept us from intentionally moving forward together as a couple.

My own experience fires my passion to share what I've learned. It's been an honor to work with couples professionally over the last 30 years—I'm filled with feelings of humility, gratitude, and compassion as I look back. The framework I present in this book will help you understand what's going on in your marriage from two angles—(1) neuroscience and (2) the Bible—so that you and your spouse can choose to move forward together toward a solid, loving, intimate marriage regardless of your starting point.

Before you begin to read through this book, I recommend taking the marital assessment at:

NakedandExposed.com/resources

The assessment will give you a window into the current state of your marriage and provide a point of reference for the material I present.

CHAPTER 1:

What Is Intimacy and Why Is It So Elusive?

. . . .

The man said, "This is now bone of my bones and
flesh of my flesh; she shall be called 'woman,' for she
was taken out of man."
That is why a man leaves his father and mother and is
united to his wife, and they become one flesh.
Adam and his wife were both naked, and they felt no shame.
GENESIS 2:23-25[1]

Sam and Jane were a great couple. They met in college, were immediately attracted to each other, and began dating. They bonded over their shared interest in athletics and the outdoors. They lived in the Midwest and enjoyed hiking together. During their long hikes, they talked for hours about their hopes, dreams, shared values, and faith.

They told each other about their experiences growing up. They came from very different backgrounds. Jane came from an intact,

1

traditional, conservative family. No one in her family had ever been divorced. Sam came from a divorced family; his dad wasn't a part of his life for much of his childhood. They wanted to be family to each other. Jane wanted to give Sam the family he never had, and he *wanted* that kind of family very much. They bonded through these conversations and dreams.

Shortly after they graduated from college, Sam and Jane got married. They set out to fulfill their dreams and ambitions, aiming to create a life of meaning and purpose. Jane wanted to go into medicine, and Sam wanted to be an entrepreneur. He hoped to use his business ventures to raise money and start a philanthropic foundation that would allow them to go into third world countries and provide medical clinics that Jane could direct.

Their vision of building a marriage and extending it to doing good in the world drew them together. They didn't think they'd be able to fulfill that mission and calling if they were apart. They had a big, beautiful church wedding and stayed in a countryside castle in France on their honeymoon. It was a fairytale start to their plans.

But then... fast forward to the more recent past. Jane got pregnant immediately after the honeymoon and never finished her medical education. They've been married for several years and now have three children. Sam has worked arduously to make his business ventures succeed, but he's had a hard time finding financial backing. He spends more time in the business and fundraising for the business than he does at home. On top of that, his mom's health has declined, his dad is out of the picture, and Sam is the only child—so they've moved his mom into their home. Now they're part of the sandwich generation—taking care of aging parents and young kids at the same time, which cuts into time for themselves individually and as a couple. They don't have time for long hikes, leisurely walks, or hours of conversation—not to mention planning the philanthropy missions they dreamed of before they got married. Life has gotten in the way. Their day-to-day obligations and the sheer exhaustion of life are straining their marriage. When I met Sam and Jane, they were fighting, disoriented, and disenchanted by their dreams of what could have been. Jane said she had no privacy in their home. Their sexual intimacy was one of the first things to go when the daily pressures of life increased. Sam's mom was demanding, and the kids were needy. She and Sam hardly ever communicated, and when they did, it always seemed to turn into an argument.

What has happened to Sam and Jane happens to many couples. Intimacy has eluded them. The deep emotional, psychological, and physical closeness they once had has faded. The safety and security they felt in their relationship, which provided a sense of emotional well- being, has disappeared. External stressors—the busyness of parenting, career demands, and Sam's mom moving in with them—have taken priority over their relationship. With their communication broken down, they have difficulty expressing their emotions to each other, and they have little time and energy to nurture their relationship and invest in rebuilding their intimacy.

Is Intimacy Sex?

Many people regard sex and intimacy as mutually interchangeable words. Intimacy, they think, is simply the act of having sex.

However, sex is a culmination of multiple levels of intimacy: knowing one another emotionally, sharing with each other mentally, and joining together in spiritual purpose. These all culminate in a physical act of nakedness and becoming one. Intimacy involves being known, on *all* levels. When we settle merely for the physical act of sex, we eliminate the oneness God designed for us across all levels. Having sex—becoming one flesh in the physical realm—is a beautiful metaphor for becoming one with our partner in many ways.

Marriage, as designed by God, started out with Adam and Eve authentic and vulnerable, completely naked and exposed. They felt safe and secure with each other. That was the original design... until everything changed. After their fall from grace, coverings and defenses came in and inhibited their original, beautiful connection. So began the decline of the intimate bond we were created for.

What is Intimacy?

Intimacy involves knowing and being known by another person. I like to break down the word intimacy like this:

in–to–me–I–see

Intimacy is letting someone see into you at levels, beyond what you allow other people to see. In an intimate relationship, you expose yourself and give feedback to your partner to deepen your understanding and knowing each other on multiple levels.

Intimacy is a multidimensional concept that encompasses the emotional, physical, and psychological closeness between partners. In a relationship, there is a beautiful dance of connection, intimacy, and renewal—a dance that is essential for fostering deep emotional bonds, sustaining a sense of closeness, and nurturing a profound sense of vitality. Intimacy requires intentional effort, honest communication, and a shared commitment to nurturing a relationship. By dedicating ourselves to these practices, we open ourselves to a world of profound possibility—a world where love deepens, intimacy flourishes, and relationships become a source of transformation and joy.

Dimensions of Intimacy

There are several dimensions of intimacy. Understanding and nurturing these dimensions leads to a more fulfilling and connected partnership.

The different types of intimacy are interconnected and may overlap. Each type contributes to the overall closeness and depth of a relationship.

Emotional intimacy involves being honest about what you're feeling. In addition, those emotions *matter* to the other person. There's a culture of care in your relationship; your empathic response to your partner demonstrates that it matters to you what they're feeling.

Mental intimacy enables you to show up with your stories and thoughts about yourself, life, and your partner. It allows you to hope and dream together, but it also permits you to protest and share likes and dislikes. You can tell each other your preferences—even preferences about each other—and there's a safe environment in the relationship so that those preferences are well-received, matter, and cause you to make adjustments for each other.

Spiritual intimacy is a matter of having a shared purpose in life. The shared purpose may involve faith or a way of worship, a set of values, or engaging in service to a cause or philanthropic endeavor.

Physical intimacy and sexual intimacy aren't necessarily the same thing. You and your spouse can be physically intimate without having sex, giving affection in other physical ways: a foot rub, a scalp massage, holding hands, hugging, and cuddling—physical contact that you know your spouse enjoys and desires.

Sexual intimacy in a healthy relationship is the overflow of the other areas of intimacy. It's a beautiful physical expression of being emotionally, mentally, and spiritually connected. Full intercourse is the culmination of the dimensions of intimacy, learning about each other's bodies and how they respond.

In order for you and your spouse to have any kind of intimacy—emotional, mental, spiritual, or physical—you need to trust one another. You each need a certain level of perceived safety and security with the other. When you have these elements, you can expose yourselves and make yourselves vulnerable.

When the dimensions of intimacy are developed in a relationship, healthy love matures and deepens into a truly intimate bond.

Sam and Jane had all of the components of intimacy when they first got married, but the stressors of life got in the way, slowly eroding their intimate bond.

Safety and security *deepen intimacy* over time

Their marriage began in a place of hope, with dreams of what they would create together. They had trust, respect, and an emotional connection that allowed them to be open and vulnerable, sharing their most intimate thoughts and deepest emotions without fear. They took time out to have fun and had a deep physical and sexual connection. They had a shared purpose and plans to be of service to Third World countries, setting up medical clinics that Jane could direct.

Safety and Security Contribute to Intimacy

Safety and security contribute to building intimacy. In romantic relationships, we need to feel safe in order to be open and vulnerable. Security involves knowing that your partner is there for you, available and responsive to your needs and wants. Together or apart, you have no fear that your bond will be disrupted. You carry thoughts of each other throughout each day, and your relationship is marked by a mutual give and take.

For Sam and Jane, the bond of safety and security broke down when Sam's mother moved in. Jane was already overstretched. She had no reprieve from her work and driving for carpools, soccer practices, and piano lessons, because Sam was always working. She was surviving, but she needed emotional support.

When she told Sam that she couldn't handle having Sam's mother move in, Sam felt betrayed. He couldn't believe she wanted to put his mom in a nursing home.

Jane also felt betrayed. She hadn't spoken up about her exhaustion stemming from Sam constantly working and not being able to share in the parenting responsibilities. Her anxiety and stress climaxed when she faced the added responsibility of caring for Sam's ailing mother—and this also made her feel guilty. She didn't want Sam to think she didn't love his mother; in fact, she *did* love her. But their communication had broken down, and it was no longer easy to express her true feelings. Each time she tried to tell Sam how she felt, he seemed to take things the wrong way, and they would end up arguing.

Their deep love they still had for each other was the catalyst that prompted them to reach out to me for help.

Many couples need intervention when the busyness of life creeps in and their communication breaks down. For Sam and Jane, busyness was routine. They were so wrapped up in obligations and responsibilities that they forgot to carve out alone time with each other.

When couples are dating or early on in a marriage, opportunities to spend time together without other responsibilities occur naturally, because they aren't as busy. Later, they need to *schedule* time and be more intentional about being together so they can continue deepening their intimate bond.

Couples that schedule time alone to be with each other on a weekly basis have more safety and security in their relationships. They understand the importance of having a renewal system. A renewal system is a set of habits that form a deliberate way to strengthen a marriage relationship and create an intimate bond that deepens over time. Couples that have a renewal system have more opportunities to be vulnerable and create intimacy. They avoid living with each other simply as business partners, co-parents, or co-household managers.

Without renewal systems, many couples lead parallel lives. Caring for kids, careers, and aging parents may eliminate their alone time altogether. Renewal systems counterbalance the stressors of life. Examples of renewal system habits include:

- Intentional date nights
- Scheduled moments alone together
- We're a team: "Hey, I've got the kids; you do the dishes," or "I'll help with homework;
- you do the cooking." Or more broadly, "I'll work, and you run the household."

A renewal system ensures the ongoing health and vitality of a marriage.

The Intimacy Formula

A relationship is like an equilateral triangle, with chemistry, companionship, and commitment each occupying a side. Each side is equally important.

Chemistry, of course, is what initially differentiates a romantic relationship from a friendship, a coworker relationship, or another family relationship. Whatever we call it—chemistry, passion, attraction—it's a magnetic attraction we feel toward that special someone.

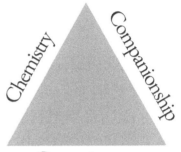

The feelings of romantic attraction are a mystery we don't fully understand. Why do we feel this way with *one* person but not *every* person? But it's important to recognize that chemistry alone *cannot* sustain a lifelong romantic attachment.

Once two people develop chemistry—a connection, an interest in love—they turn a corner and develop the *companionship* side of the triangle. They might start asking:

- Do we enjoy each other's company?
- Do we have shared likes and dislikes?
- Do we have shared values, goals, and dreams?
- Do we enjoy shared recreational or leisure activities?

Companionship, or friendship, develops along these lines, beyond infatuation or initial attraction. It involves a sense of closeness and emotional connection that goes beyond chemistry. Companionship involves enjoying each other's company,

10

being there for one another, and supporting each other with understanding and advice. Companions have a deep sense of joy in being together. Companionship is the backbone of a strong and fulfilling romantic relationship.

Commitment is the third leg of the triangle. When people commit to each other, they ensure safety and security in their relationship by pledging to be exclusive to one another.

The three sides of this relationship triangle are interdependent; they prop each other up and enable the development of more mature love.

> In marriage, the *commitment* we make with our willing vows is until *death do us part*

When your relationship stands on all three legs of the triangle, you'll have relationship satisfaction and longevity. A relationship built on chemistry, companionship, and commitment provides safety and security. Safety and security, in turn, deepen intimacy over time.

To deepen their intimate bond, partners need to perceive each other as loving, accepting, available, and responsive to physical, mental, emotional, and spiritual needs and longings.

Now, let's consider four things that erode safety and security and work against the deepening of intimacy.

Four Things That Destroy Intimacy

As couples dance apart and a chasm opens between them, their feelings of safety and security erode. They shift from wanting to please each other to feeling obligated to show up in the relationship. These changes don't happen overnight; intimacy eludes many couples through an unintentional slide down a gradual, slippery slope—a slide that usually involves one or more of the following four factors:

1. *Inattention*

Inattention—that is, not paying attention to each other—is the first factor that degrades the safety and security of a marriage. Let's illustrate.

Sam and Jane, when discussing the stressors and busyness of their schedules, decide there is no time for their date night. It seems that their protected time was always squished out by the urgent. Over time, it became a non-issue and fell off their radar of priorities. The busyness of life has left them limited space to connect. Chronic unprioritized attention or a lackadaisical attitude toward their relationship investment erodes their intimate bond.

2. *Betrayal Wounds and Unresolved Pain Points*

When one partner betrays the other's trust, the betrayal inflicts deep emotional pain and breaks their intimate bond. Betrayal wounds or unresolved pain points in a relationship come from experiences that hurt one of the partners. Secrecy, lying, affairs, addiction, and anger outbursts, to name a few produce wounds and pain points that can have a significant effect on trust and safety in a relationship. If your partner betrays you and there isn't any healing from the ensuing emotional and mental pain, the unresolved wound will put emotional and physical distance between you.

When couples don't address betrayal wounds and pain points, the unaddressed wounds will continue to resurface again and again at triggering moments which hinders healing. Naturally, we don't like to talk about our wounds. In some instances, we don't know *how* to talk about them. So, instead of addressing our wounds, we sweep them all under the rug. Over time, the lump under the rug becomes more and more noticeable. We don't know how or are unwilling to address these pains in a soft and vulnerable way, so.they go unaddressed. Often, they emerge as a secondary emotion—anger. Many times, we don't know how to respond to wounds our partners received in the relationship, because it's hard for us to accept our partners not seeing us or painting us in a good light.

Consequently, we avoid owning our part of the pain and making changes to create a safer and more secure relationship.

3. *Family of Origin*

Your family of origin is where you grew up. It typically consists of parents, primary caregivers, and siblings. Our family of origin plays a significant role in shaping our beliefs, values, and behaviors. All of us have vulnerabilities and sensitivities from our family of origin. We form our ideas of what a romantic relationship should look like based on our childhood experiences. Our parents raised us and taught us how to love, interact with others, and form emotional attachments to people. We transfer this background into our adult romantic relationships. The attachments we had with our primary caregivers pave the way for our emotional attachments with romantic partners. We will delve deeper into how our family of origin affects intimacy in Chapter 3. Without us even knowing, our family of origin has an effect on the way we interact and create that intimate romantic bond.

4. *Rigid, Chronic Argument Cycles*

A rigid, chronic argument cycle in a marriage is a repetitive pattern of unproductive arguments. It's healthy for couples to have disagreements, but disagreements should be brought to a resolution. A cycle of unresolved disagreements can become deeply ingrained in a relationship and lead to ongoing conflict and emotional distress.

In Sam and Jane's case, the pattern was that Sam walked away, and Jane screamed. Over time, as the cycle evolved, Jane saw Sam as unloving and unresponsive; Sam saw Jane as unreasonable and emotionally unstable. When they were first married, they couldn't have imagined not wanting to show up for each other in ways that create connection and resolve conflict, but that's where they found themselves. Their intimate bond was broken by a rigid, chronic argument cycle that caused them to lose the feeling of wanting to be there for each other.

Let's face it—couples have disagreements. We can use disagreements to deepen our intimate relationships and get to know each other better. Negative fight cycles prevent couples from working through their disagreements. Eventually, such cycles also prevent couples from reasonably protesting things they don't like, because any protest turns into an argument. When a couple is stuck in a negative fight cycle, their internal narratives about each other change—they no longer perceive each other as safe, secure, loving, accepting, available, and responsive. Perceptions shift from where they were when they said "I do" at the altar, changing how they show up in the relationship—affecting their emotions, motivation (*wanting* to please each other), and behavior. The more chronic and rigid a fight cycle becomes, the more it reinforces a couple's new, negative perceptions of each other. When spouses recognize a decline in their desire to please one another, the negative effects compound. Of these, the negative fight cycle is the biggest culprit of relationship dissatisfaction, erosion of intimacy and can be the greatest predictor of divorce. [2]

When Sam and Jane first reached out to me, they were in crisis. They had gone to a secular counselor—and it helped a little bit. But they soon fell back into their fight cycle. Their communication was nonexistent, and they weren't a team at all. They went to their pastor to ask for recommendations and ended up coming to me. Sam and Jane were drawn to my intensive counseling program, because between their three kids and their businesses, they couldn't keep up with weekly counseling sessions.

Typically, when husbands hear about the intensive model, they picture a grueling 16-hour session with their wife and a therapist. But as I guided the conversation, Sam opened up like a faucet. As he spoke, he saw how well his wife was responding to what he was saying, so he opened up more and shared things he'd never told her before. They discovered things about each other they hadn't learned in fourteen years of marriage. They learned how to communicate in a whole new way.

Now, they're better than they've ever been. They've come together as a team and as a family. They understand each other so much more now that they know each other's triggers and communication styles.

Sam learned that most of his wounds came from growing up in a turbulent household. His dad lived a wild lifestyle while his mom tried to hold things together; eventually, they divorced. Sam learned that he doesn't like chaos, because that was all he experienced growing up; he likes structure. With three kids and his ailing mother in their home, things were often chaotic. He used to retreat not only from the chaos of the three kids but also from his marriage; now he knows that he can just step out of the room and take a moment to regroup.

Jane learned how to empathize with Sam. She learned that asking curious questions rather than demanding or attacking leads to a deeper level of connection. By the end of their intensive, they understood each other without any rage or ego.

What couples like Sam and Jane really want is to be known, understood, and seen amid the stressors and chaos of life. They want a connection where they can be vulnerable and empathetic.

Suppose a couple has safety and security in their relationship. When something happens to bring in uncertainty, they can communicate to understand how each of them is feeling. Today, in stressful moments, Jane feels safe revealing her thoughts to Sam. Sam is able to listen and reassure Jane, offering her the security she needs and deepening their intimate bond.

> Safety and security are built by being *loving, accepting, available,* and *responsive* to one another

I tell couples that they need a lily pad; that's where they reside together as an *us*. Your lily pad is where you and your partner become one; it's where you do life together, experience warmth and fun. The lily pad is only big enough for the two of you. I will be discussing more about the lily pad later.

At the beginning of a relationship, we get butterflies—a feeling of excitement and anticipation when we see our partner. We need that initial connection in order to plan when and how to see each other and, as things progress, realize that this person is *the* one—of all the people of the opposite gender on the planet, this is the one I choose to be with for the rest of my life. At the altar, we willingly offer ourselves to our spouses, and we can't imagine a day when we wouldn't want to try to make them happy.

That's the starting point—you and your spouse camping out on your own lily pad together. As life goes on, your intimate bond is challenged. If you're able to maintain safety and security in your marriage—being vulnerable and exposed, listening and giving feedback—your intimate bond will grow and deepen.

CHAPTER REFLECTION:

 To counter the erosion of intimacy in your marriage, be aware of the stories you tell yourself about your spouse. Be intentional about those stories—revisit the love, passion, and butterflies you felt at the beginning of your love story. Create time to go through your wedding photos or reminisce about your proposal story together.

CHAPTER 2:

From Desire to Obligation: Shifting Attitudes

. . . .

Dear children, let us not love with words or speech
but with actions and in truth.
This is how we know that we belong to the truth and
how we set our hearts at rest in his presence.
1 JOHN 3:18-19

Bud and Cindy came to me in a crisis. They rated their relationship at a seven out of ten, but they were on diverging paths. Fortunately, their pastor recommended that they see me. They didn't consider divorce to be an option, and they were willing to fight for each other.

When they first got married, they were fiercely independent. In their premarital counseling, they hadn't realized how their independence molded their character. After having a child and weathering the Covid-19 pandemic, they realized they needed each other but, they didn't know how to be there for each other. They entered into marriage eager to fulfill their vows and do all kinds of things for each other, but over time their attitude of desire became one of obligation.

At the marriage altar, two individuals come together publicly to declare their love and commitment to each other. They exchange vows expressing their deep devotion to each other, marking the beginning of a lifelong journey.

Voluntary marriage vows signify a genuine desire to enter into the sacred union of marriage. They reflect a profound emotional investment in the marriage relationship and demonstrate an intimate bond of love, passion, and commitment, embracing the responsibilities and joys that come with marriage.

There is a *contractual* aspect to marriage—signing the marriage license. But you don't *sign* your vows. You *offer* to do those things, willingly. The contractual commitment that couples make establishes a legal framework that protects each party's rights and interests and lays out the responsibilities they have toward each other in the marriage. It is a legally binding agreement.

But the marriage contract doesn't define the emotional and personal aspects of the relationship. Marriage involves more than just a legal contract. It is a partnership based on love, trust, and emotional connection. Yet over time, many couples shift from voluntary commitment—*wanting* to please each other—to a sense of obligation.

Bud and Cindy had once been deeply in love. Their marriage had blossomed with desire, passion, and dreams of a shared future. But as the years passed, they drifted apart.

Bud, once an adventurous soul, was trapped in the routine of his job, drowning in deadlines and endless meetings. Cindy's dedication to motherhood left her little time for self-care or personal pursuits. They once were vibrant, independent individuals—but those people seemed lost, buried beneath layers of responsibility and obligation.

However, amid the growing apathy, a glimmer of hope remained. Bud stumbled on some old photos that reminded him of the love and happiness they once shared. He opened up to Cindy about his feelings of disconnection and longing. To his surprise, Cindy said she felt the same way and confessed her own desires for a revitalized relationship. Both of them had been silently yearning for change, but fear and inertia held them back.

I have no doubt that Bud and Cindy were madly in love when they made their marriage vows. But when I met them, they had lost their desire to please each other. My job was to help them change the stories they were telling themselves about each other—stories that were very different from when they fell in love. To restore their desire to care for each other, they needed to remember the beginning of their story. They had been so excited to begin their life together. Now, they were willing to do whatever they needed to do to restore their desire to be there for each other.

If you feel like your marriage is a duty, how do you restore the beautiful state of wanting to be everything to each other?

That's where Bud and Cindy found themselves. When I work with couples in conflict, I often wonder, "How did they get here?"

The Internal Narrative

Couples create narratives—stories in their heads—about each other that help them make sense of the dynamics of their relationships.

Our internal narratives are shaped by our perceptions and interpretations of our partners' behaviors and actions. Consider these illustrations:

- **The perfect partner:** Our partner should be the perfect companion that can do no wrong.
- **The mind reader:** We know what our partner is thinking or feeling without any need for clear communication, and they should know as well. As a result, we make assumptions about their intentions or interpret their actions based on our own biases and insecurities.

Although the stories we tell ourselves often *don't* reflect reality, they can and do shape our attitudes, behaviors, and expectations.

Bud and Cindy's internal narratives shifted little by little, slowly eroding their desire to fulfill their wedding vows. Each had stories in their head about the other that shaped their relationship. I needed to bring them back to the original story, to rediscover who they fell in love with.

Cindy asked me to teach her how to speak Bud's language. She wanted to know how to read the signals he was *actually* sending as opposed to the stories playing out in her head: Bud didn't care, Bud had lost his desire for her. In our sessions, Cindy learned that she was a *fighter* and Bud was a *freezer*. In a conflict, freezers retreat, fighters confront. When Bud and Cindy clashed, Bud stayed quiet or left the room. He hated confrontation, so he always retreated, leaving Cindy to feel as though she was the only one fighting for their marriage. Cindy learned that she had to fight *with* Bud and not *against* him. Bud learned that he needed to communicate with Cindy in a way that helped them connect. Through our sessions together, they learned how to work through stressful times.

Bud and Cindy embarked on a journey of rediscovery. They made a conscious effort to prioritize their relationship, carving out quality time for each other and engaging in shared activities that reignited their passion. Slowly, the walls that had separated them crumbled. They discovered new depths of understanding, compassion, and forgiveness.

Bud and Cindy breathed new life into their marriage. They reignited their desire for each other and built a deep, enduring love—one that transcended obligation. They realized that marriage requires ongoing effort and a willingness to evolve together. Their love had been tested, but it emerged stronger, reminding them that even in the face of challenges, love can be restored.

From Desire to Obligation

When a newly married couple begins their life together, they're full of excitement, love, and anticipation. These feelings drive their commitment to nurture a deep and intimate bond, creating a desire to be there for each other. They prioritize open communication, emotional connection, and shared goals, cultivating a strong foundation of trust and mutual support. Their desire to create a fulfilling and lasting partnership fuels their efforts to maintain their intimate bond, fostering growth and resilience in the face of challenges.

But sometimes life gets in the way. Couples gradually lose their "want to"; their desire for each other begins to fade. External pressures, complacency, and unmet expectations chip away at their "want to." The focus shifts from nurturing their relationship to fulfilling duties, leading to a sense of detachment. A lack of intentional communication, inattention, unresolved pain points, emotional disconnection, and fight cycles eat away at their intimate bond.

But couples can restore that intimate bond. Renewing your commitment to each other, fostering empathy, and actively engaging in the desire of love and partnership, you can rekindle your intimate bond and rediscover the joy and fulfillment that brought you together in the first place.

Bud and Cindy were strongly committed to their marriage. They sought out premarital counseling to begin with a good foundation. When their relationship was rocky, they didn't want to divorce; they were willing to fight for their marriage. By working with me, they adjusted their attitudes and rekindled their intimate bond.

> Over time, couples *lose* the feeling of "*want to*" to be there for each other

Premarital counseling and counseling for couples in conflict are distinct types of counseling that serve very different purposes.

I work with couples in all stages: newly engaged couples, couples that have already secured divorce attorneys or separated, and everything in between. There's a stark difference in the way a newly engaged couple and a couple that's planning a divorce walk through the doors of my counseling practice.

Typically, a couple coming for premarital counseling arrives together, often in the same car, a few minutes early. They're holding hands, whispering, and giggling. They're excited to be there, anticipating the things they're going to learn. In the counseling room, they move the pillows from the center of the couch to the sides so they can sit together in the middle. They sit with their sides touching, and they have a deer-in-the-headlights look of total bliss. They're about to start their life together and are excited for their coming adventures.

Couples in conflict often arrive separately. They often stagger their arrival times, so they don't have to sit with each other in the lobby. When they come into my office, they look at the ground rather than at each other. They move the pillows to the *center* of the couch, creating a barrier between them so they can sit as far apart as possible. You can cut the tension with a knife.

When I work with couples in conflict, I try to bring them back to when they were over the moon just to be near their partner.

Shifting Attitudes

One of the joys of marriage counseling is seeing a couple's attitudes shift, seeing them move from obligation back to desire. Making this shift requires introspection, open communication, and intentional effort.

For example, Bud and Cindy were committed to restoring their marriage. They took time to reflect on their current attitudes toward each other. They identified the underlying reasons that dragged their marriage into the realm of obligation.

They reflected on what initially attracted them and what they appreciated about each other. They expressed gratitude and complimented each other, nurturing a positive and loving atmosphere.

They prioritized the emotional connection—something they had lost—and began to build it back. They took time to engage in activities that fostered their connection. They planned quality time together.

They learned how to communicate in ways that made both of them comfortable and allowed them to be vulnerable with each other.

They had been living parallel lives; now, they made time for points of intersection, making sure that their time together deepened their intimacy.

They learned to be intentional in their conversation—things like a quick, "I love you."

Now, they feel like they're prepared for anything that comes their way—including things that are out of their control. They believe they're meant to get through anything together and know that they wouldn't be able to do it with anyone else.

What happened to Bud and Cindy can happen to anyone. Couples start out loving, accepting, available, and responsive. But as life goes on, they start to show up differently—they become less available or not as loving. Their internal narratives shift. Although our internal stories may not reflect reality, what we continuously tell ourselves in our head can change a relationship and erode intimate bonds.

If you're in this situation and you want a different result, one of the first things you need to do is look at the stories you're telling yourself about your spouse and endeavor to restore them to the thoughts and feelings you had when you committed to each other.

In the next chapter, we'll look at the problem from another angle—neuroscience and attachment theory.

CHAPTER REFLECTION:

 Write out the story you tell yourself about your spouse. Deliberately write out the new narrative that shifts your warm emotions back. We have the capacity to have both. Intentionally revisit this new narrative daily.

CHAPTER 3:

Neuroscience: How Brain Biology Affects Your Relationships

. . . .

I praise you because I am fearfully and wonderfully made;
your works are wonderful.

PSALM 139:14

Jim and Mary have been married for eighteen years and have six kids between the ages of three and twenty-one. Their lives are incredibly busy. Last year, they got stuck in a cycle of arguments, and they couldn't resolve any of their conflicts. Before that, they had worked so well as a team in careers, parenting, and ministry. So, they were really caught off guard by all of this happening in their marriage.

In their fight cycle, Jim would break away and Mary would chase after him. They couldn't figure out why it was happening. How did their intimate bond dissolve so quickly? They came to me for a few counseling sessions that got them back on track for a month or so, but then they fell back into the same fight cycle. So, they decided to do a couples intensive with me.

In a couple's intensive, a couple works with me for several hours a day for two or three days in a row. An intensive provides the equivalent of six months of outpatient counseling.

When Jim and Mary arrived for their intensive, they were in a bad place. They both had grown up with divorced parents. They had committed to not getting divorced; they didn't want their children growing up in a divorced household. They had worked diligently in their marriage, but somehow, something had shifted.

We needed to find the root of their problem. I explained to them how family of origin and brain biology can affect our relationships.

The Brain's Connection to Romantic Love

As unlikely as it may sound, the brain and neuroscience play a significant part in our romantic attachments—not only in the disconnect cycles you and your partner experience but also in your feelings of passion and romance.

When we're attracted to someone, a chemical reaction occurs in the brain—a biological force that helps create feelings of pleasure, euphoria, and attachment.

Jim and Mary were in a disconnect cycle: Their fight cycle created emotional distance between them that had a deep effect on their communication and intimacy. In a disconnect cycle, communication breaks down, resulting in repeated misunderstandings, conflict, and emotional distance. Poor listening, defensiveness, blaming, a lack of empathy, criticism, and emotional withdrawal are all part of a disconnect cycle. Without intervention, a disconnect cycle can become ingrained in our brain and hard to break resulting in a dance with the same steps, moves and themes.

What follows is a brief overview of the neuroscience related to relationships. Don't let the word *neuroscience* frighten you. Romantic love isn't just a thought, feeling, poem, or fantasy. It has a biological foundation.

Neuroscience 101

The **nervous system** is composed of your brain, spinal cord, and the nerves that run throughout your body. It conveys signals from the brain to the rest of the body, keeping you alive and allowing you to act based on your thoughts.

Two distinct regions of the brain—regions that are important to our discussion—are the cerebral cortex and the cerebellum. I'll refer to them in terms of their general anatomical orientation— the cerebral cortex is your **front brain**, and the cerebellum is your **back brain**.

Our *autonomic* nervous system—the part that does things *automatically*—also consists of two parts:

1. The **parasympathetic** nervous system controls essential functions like breathing and the beating of our heart.

2. The **sympathetic** nervous system—the brain's survival mechanism—assesses danger and triggers our fight, flight, or freeze responses.

The parasympathetic and sympathetic nervous systems are complementary; they work together to keep us alive and safe, adapting constantly to our changing circumstances.

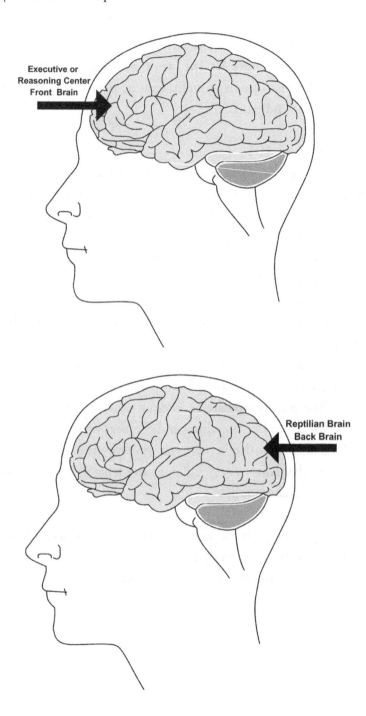

Executive or
Reasoning Center
Front Brain

Reptilian Brain
Back Brain

The **prefrontal cortex** is the part of the cerebral cortex (the front brain) that operates consciously and deliberately. It's responsible for abstract reasoning and the development of spiritual, moral, and ethical beliefs. It also handles problem solving, conflict management, and emotional intelligence.

Take a moment to be quiet and listen to your surroundings. What do you hear? Do you hear voices in another room? Do you hear birds outside the window? Do you hear a clock ticking?

This exercise illustrates how your front brain grounds you in the present moment through your five senses: sight, sound, smell, taste, and touch.

When you're in the *right now*, you're in your front brain.

The **cerebellum** (your back brain) is responsible for movement, balance, and language. It is also referred to as the *reptilian* brain because it is the area of the brain that controls instinctual thinking and survival. The reptilian brain controls our fight, flight, or freeze responses when we perceive a threat.

When you're in your back brain, your body continues operating, but your mind may be somewhere else. For example, you pull into the driveway after commuting home from work, and you think, *Wait a minute, how did I get home?* Did I go through that intersection?

Was it a red light? Was it a green light?

As you were driving, perhaps you replayed a conversation from earlier in the day. Perhaps you were thinking about the to-do list waiting for you as soon as you walk in the front door.

Your back brain, your autopilot, took over and got you home. The subconscious processing of your back brain helps you carry out routine activities without awareness (e.g., driving home from work). The back brain relies on stored information and established neural pathways to execute behaviors automatically.

How do the front brain and back brain coordinate? The back brain is always on, and it's a fast operating system. Why? If you walk into a dark room and your back brain detects *danger,* it kicks in immediately to protect you: your eyes dilate and your respiration increases. However, your front brain kicks in and informs the back brain of more contextual information.

This is your house. You used your own key to get in the door. Just turn on the lights.

The front brain regulates the back brain; it shuts down the fight, flight, or freeze response. The front brain tells the back brain what to do with sensory input; it makes sense of your surroundings.

With this background, let's look at how the brain develops and how its development affects our relationships.

The Brain's Emotional Development

The brain develops from the base of the skull to the front of the skull over the course of infancy, childhood, and young adulthood. Barring the effects of drugs and alcohol and being dropped on your head, the prefrontal cortex (front brain) finally finishes developing between the ages of 21 and 25. Research suggests that there is a higher rate of divorce among couples that marry before the age of 25 compared to those who marry later.[1]

In other words, abstract reasoning isn't fully developed in humans until they hit 25. That's also the age at which you have the full

> The brain doesn't *fully develop* until age 21-25 years which can have some *implications* for couples who marry at an *early age*

capacity to solidify your moral, ethical, and spiritual beliefs. Before we hit 25, we mostly believe what we've been taught to believe. Jim and Mary got married at 25. They were intentional about their marriage and tried to establish a healthy foundation. But they didn't realize how the neuroscience of their emotional development would affect their romantic attachment.

The brain's emotional development occurs in a series of stages, and each stage is characterized by distinct changes and milestones.

The Stages of Emotional Development

Babies' emotions begin to develop from infancy. Newborns experience emotions such as love, joy, and fear and rely on their caregivers to comfort and soothe them. They have their first experiences of **moving from emotional deregulation to emotional regulation**.

Emotional deregulation is a state of struggling to manage our emotions. Emotional regulation occurs when we become aware of an emotion, understand it, and express it in a socially appropriate way. Emotional deregulation and regulation are a normal part of brain development.

A caretaker is an important person in a baby's life—for instance, a mother caring for her son. The mother begins the process of taking her baby from emotional deregulation to emotional regulation. She takes care of her son's needs, scheduling when he eats and sleeps and providing emotional support.

Suppose the baby feels scared or anxious. His mother responds by picking him up, speaking softly, and providing gentle reassurance. Her presence and calming actions help regulate his emotions. This emotional co-regulation enables him to learn how to self-soothe and manage his emotions.

The next stage of emotional development is **moving from mistrust to trust**. In this stage, infants manifest separation anxiety. The baby looks around the room and realizes, *I'm all alone.* He begins to cry. When his cries are heard, his mother comes and consoles him, making him feel safe.

Moving from dependence to independence is another important stage in emotional development. Suppose the baby is at a playground. He's laughing and giggling and playing, but occasionally, he looks back to see if his mother is there. When he makes eye contact with her and she smiles at him, he continues to play. But if he looks back and doesn't see his mother, he deregulates, he can't laugh or play. His back brain activates his fight, flight, or freeze response. He might yell, "Mommy!" and run around looking for her. Or he might cry and wait for her to respond. When his mother is present, he feels secure. With a secure foundation of attachment, he learns to explore his surroundings confidently, and this develops independence.

The safety and security that primary caregivers provide co-regulate our stress responses and create a bond in which emotional development matures. This results in higher-order emotional capacities such as empathy, stress tolerance, and self-esteem.

Physically, brain development requires appropriate nutrition, rest, recreation, and stimulation. The brain's emotional development requires the ingredients of love, acceptance, availability, and responsiveness from our primary caregivers. If our primary caregivers provide these elements throughout our developmental years the majority of the time, we tend to do well emotionally. In contrast, if our primary caregivers are consistently absent or unresponsive, the emotional co-regulation process is disrupted, leading to a sense of insecurity and mistrust. An extended lack of emotional co-regulation can impact our emotional development and our ability to form secure relationships later in life.

The attachment system between babies and their primary caregivers plays a critical role in emotional co-regulation. Through consistent and responsive caregiving, caregivers create a safe and secure emotional environment, allowing children to develop trust and emotional skills. These early experiences of emotional co-regulation set the foundation for healthy emotional development and the ability to form secure relationships as adults.

The human brain is a complex organ that operates by way of coordination between the front and back regions—front brain and back brain. However, with regard to emotional development, the brain is specifically designed and hardwired to co-regulate in coordination with primary caregivers. For example, co-regulation occurs when a parent steps in and soothes a baby, helping the baby process emotion. Such co-regulation is essential for our survival and overall emotional development.

Are you starting to see the brain's connection to romantic love?

Our Emotional Memories

Deep in our brain, there is a place called the **amygdala** where we store negative emotional memories—times when we didn't feel safe and secure.

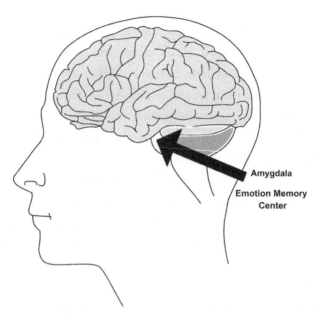

Amygdala
Emotion Memory
Center

The amygdala is part of the **limbic system**. The limbic system doesn't work in isolation but works together with the front brain, back brain, and sensory processing areas of the brain to regulate and interpret emotions and regulate behaviors.

The amygdala (which I call "Amy" for short) is a key player in the brain's emotional development and the processing of emotions because it's where conscious or unconscious memories of when important people were not there for us.

It's strange to think that God would want us to remember feeling unloved or unaccepted or when important people weren't available or responsive to us. Why is it important to remember those things?

When you touch a hot stove and get burned, the pain you feel reminds you not to touch fire. Our emotional memories stored in the amygdala function the same way—we remember so we'll avoid similar situations in the future. Our negative emotional memories serve a protective function.

The human body responds to emotional threats much like physical threats. Think about how you feel when you look over the edge of a cliff. You feel something visceral—what I call a sucker punch moment—as your body screams *Danger! Danger! Danger!* When we experience an emotional threat—perhaps someone significant acting unloving toward us—our body has the same sucker punch response. If the pattern repeats, our amygdala draws on past experience to warn us *Danger! Danger! Danger!* In such moments, our back brain takes over, triggering a fight, flight, or freeze response.

Repeated patterns of experience create neural pathways in our brain, connections between neurons that allow information to be transmitted and processed. Pathways that are activated repeatedly form patterns of response to what's happening around us. A well-known neuroscience maxim states, "Neurons that fire together wire together." If they're repeated often enough, these reactions become rapid and rigid, bypassing reason. They're detached from executive function, moral beliefs, and present evidence.

For example, the feeling of being unloved activates the amygdala and triggers a fight response. If this pattern is repeated often enough, *fighting* becomes a habitual response to feeling unloved. The more a pattern recurs, the more it solidifies. When the pattern is triggered by our significant other, we don't use any front-brain functions; that is, we don't reason, and we may say and do things that are unreasonable. We may act contrary to our moral, ethical, and spiritual beliefs. We may be intolerant, with no capacity for empathy. We may become so impacted, our sleep and eating patterns may become deregulated.

This remarkable physiological mechanism governs our response to various situations. Understanding how this mechanism works sheds light on the patterns we see in our interactions with our spouses.

Fight, Flight, or Freeze

The fight, flight, or freeze response is a major aspect of how the amygdala's emotional memory affects our relationships. Perceiving a threat activates the body's stress response system, coordinated by the amygdala. The fight, flight, or freeze response is a primal survival instinct that evolved to protect us from potential threats in our environment.

The **fight** response prepares us to confront a threat head-on. It triggers a surge of adrenaline that energizes us, increases alertness, and readies us to defend ourselves or our loved ones.

The **flight** response prepares us to escape a threat. It activates the release of stress hormones, increases our heart rate and blood flow to our muscles, and primes us to flee from danger.

The **freeze** response puts us into a state of immobility and increased vigilance when we recognize that fighting or fleeing is impossible or unsafe. When we freeze, we enter a heightened state of alertness, remaining still and quiet in an attempt to blend into our surroundings and avoid detection.

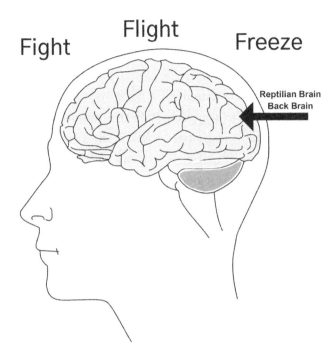

These primal responses—deeply ingrained survival instincts—are automatic and occur without conscious control. They're activated by various situations, including conflicts or threats within our relationships. When a situation with our partner touches our memories of emotional hurt, of being unloved or feeling ignored, we experience a sucker punch moment. We fight, flee, or freeze, and that may create a sucker punch moment for our partner, too.

Consequently, many couples consistently argue while governed by their back brains. The fight, flight, or freeze response hijacks their ability to effectively communicate and connect. For example, during an argument

- The **fight** response results in anger or defensiveness, escalating the conflict.
- The **flight** response results in avoidance or withdrawal, creating emotional distance between partners.

• The **freeze** response results in an emotional shutdown, making productive dialogue difficult.

Jim and Mary were caught in a fight cycle dominated by the back brain. In Jim, the amygdala took over emotional processing and initiated the fight response. In Mary, the amygdala took over and initiated the flight or freeze response. They not only fought constantly; they couldn't resolve anything, because their back brain rather than the reasonable front brain dominated their conflicts. Eventually, they became hypervigilant and unsure of one another. Over time, this caused their desire for one another to ebb.

> We have a patterned response of *fight, flight* or *freeze* in response to our partner's perceived emotional threat of not being *loving, accepting, available* or *responsive*

This pattern of conflict reinforced itself in ingrained neural pathways; when sucker punch moments came, it grew harder and harder for Jim and Mary to get out of their back brains. This prevented them from accessing front-brain problem-solving and conflict-management skills. They did not have the ability to co-regulate emotionally for each other.

They started questioning their relationship.

"I love Mary," Jim said. "I'm just not sure I'm in love with her anymore."

"In the beginning of our relationship, we couldn't keep our hands off each other," Mary said.

"Now? I can take it or leave it. I don't want to have sex with Jim." Mary's tone was angry.

Constant arguing killed the passion in their marriage, so much so that they were sleeping in separate rooms. Their rigid, ingrained fight cycle resulted in more and more frequent arguments that started more and more quickly.

The Connection Between Our Primary Caregiver and How We Relate to Our Romantic Partner

Input from a primary caregiver's front brain helps an infant or child regulate the threat response of their back brain as their brain develops.

1. A need for care, comfort, or protection activates their threat response.
2. They signal the activation of the threat response by crying.
3. The primary caregiver comes to them and provides regulation in the form of soothing or care.

This attachment system is a hardwired, built-in biological system. Without it, infants wouldn't survive. Although the attachment system is critical in childhood, the need to co-regulate with another doesn't vanish in adulthood.

The Bible says we are to leave our father and mother and cleave to our spouse.

We transfer the attachment we develop with our primary caregiver to our romantic partnership. Co-regulation between spouses is similar to the co-regulation between a parent and a child. We are hardwired to

The *attachment* that we have to our primary caregiver *leaves* and *cleaves* to our romantic partner co-regulate with someone emotionally and physically to establish a safe haven, a secure base from which we can go out and explore the world. In a marriage, co-regulation is fostered by love, acceptance, availability, and responsiveness to one another.

Attachment Science

Understanding the brain's emotional development lays the foundation for understanding *attachment theory*, a psychological framework that explores the emotional bonds and relationships formed between individuals, particularly during infancy and early childhood. How we perceive safety and security in our relationships hearkens back to what we've experienced in our most loving relationships. Attachment theory emphasizes the crucial role of primary caregivers in shaping an individual's emotional development and capacity for forming secure relationships, especially with our spouses.

Over time, you transfer the role of co-regulator from your primary caregiver to your romantic partner. Consequently, you seek your partner's support, reaching out to them when you have emotional needs. You express discontent if it seems like your partner is emotionally or physically distant. The co-regulation you developed with your primary caregiver in childhood provided reassurance, trust, autonomy, and empathy; now, your partner provides these things.

When we feel uncertain about our partner, we experience emotional distress, a sucker punch. Your spouse, as the most significant person in your life, can activate the amygdala in your limbic brain, triggering distress signals. Why? Because your connection and emotional regulation with your spouse is as pivotal and essential as your connection with your primary caregivers once was. The connection between romantic love and attachment theory is backed by substantial scientific research. The attachment styles we develop with our primary caregivers in childhood persist in our adult romantic relationships and our approach to God. Attachment style also plays a significant role in how satisfied we are with our relationships.

Attachment theory was developed by John Bowlby, a British psychiatrist and psychologist. According to attachment theory, human beings have an innate and biologically based need for close emotional bonds with others, especially in times of distress. The attachment system that develops between parent and child is believed to be an evolutionary adaptation that promotes survival, protection, and support.[2]

> All of us from cradle to grave are *happiest* when life is organized...from the secure base provided by our *attachment figures*
>
> -John Bowlby

Bowlby theorized that early childhood experiences with primary caregivers impact psychological functioning throughout life. He asserted that infants are born with an internal biological mechanism that protects the caretaker–infant relationship, giving them greater chances of survival and aiding development. He referred to this mechanism as an *attachment system*.

Attachment Patterns

There are two broad attachment patterns: secure attachment and insecure attachment. Insecure attachment can be further subdivided into three additional attachment patterns: anxious, avoidant, and disorganized. Thus, there are four main attachment styles:

1. Secure
2. Anxious

3. Avoidant
4. Disorganized

1. *Secure Attachment*

If the partners in a marital relationship have a strong and healthy emotional bond full of trust, intimacy, and a sense of security, we say that they are *securely attached*. Attachment theory is built on two premises a safe haven and a secure base. Safe haven of coregulation and secure base of certainty in which to give ability to explore the world. In other words, a soft place to fall and a certain foundation to go out into the world from.

Couples with insecure attachment patterns have a negative dynamic in their relationship.

The following are considered **Insecure Attachment** patterns:

2. *Anxious Attachment*

People who are anxiously attached engage in heightened pursuit of their partners when they need reassurance of safety in the relationship. When things seem unsafe, their protests escalate. In addition, their protests are usually very prickly and, consequently, counterproductive in terms of causing their partners to meet their need for safety and security. The purpose of protest systems (which we'll cover in detail in Chapter 4) is reconnection. The protest systems of anxiously attached people are often ineffective. They struggle with self-regulation, so they reach for their partners for co-regulation in stressful moments. However, the way they reach out—their protest system—makes it challenging for their partner to move toward them.

3. *Avoidant Attachment*

Avoidant attached people tend to shut down when they feel a lack of safety and security. Instead of reaching for their partner, they withdraw and attempt to regulate their emotions and stress levels on their own.

Unfortunately, many couples include an anxiously attached partner and an avoidant attached partner. When the anxiously attached partner feels a lack of safety and security, they pursue their avoidant partner for reassurance in a prickly way. The avoidant partner needs to shut down and move away to feel safe, making it difficult for spouse to reach them emotionally. This negatively reinforces the anxious partner's sense of lacking safety, prompting them to escalate their pursuit of the avoidant partner—who, in turn, shuts down even more.

4. *Disorganized Attachment*

Disorganized attached people have unpredictable protest systems; they sometimes escalate conflicts and are sometimes dismissive. They don't use their partners as a resource for regulating emotions, and many times they don't have the capacity to regulate their own emotions. In other words, they lack both self-regulation and co-regulation skills.

| | | *Ability to Self Regulate* | |
		Yes	No
Ability to Reach for CoRegulation	Yes	Secure	Anxious
	No	Avoidant	Disorganized

Attachment Patterns in Action

During my work with Jim and Mary, I observed that Mary had an anxious attachment style. She worried when Jim had to work late and didn't respond promptly to her texts. When he came home, she typically greeted him angrily, because she believed he was distant and late because he wasn't prioritizing her. She thought Jim neither loved her nor wanted to be at home.

"You ignore me throughout the day," Mary told him. "You don't even care that I am home alone caring for our family. Coming home late is disrespectful to me."

Despite Jim's attempts to reassure her that he'd been tied up in meetings, Mary wasn't reassured. They frequently argued over her claims that Jim didn't love her as she sought heightened validation of his love.

Jim, on the other hand, had an avoidant attachment pattern. He reacted to Mary's persistent complaints by tuning her out. On the surface, he didn't seem to be affected by her emotional distress. When he offered reassurance, it came across as hollow and emotionless. He found it easier to work if he silenced his phone; that way, he didn't have to field interruptions from Mary. Some nights, he managed to calm her anger. However, he eventually slept in the guest bedroom more and more often to enjoy an evening of quiet and solitude.

"I just keep failing to make her happy," Jim told me. "I feel so inadequate. I don't know how to be the man or husband she wants. I really don't ask for much in this relationship. I work and provide for the family, but I feel so unappreciated."

Jim and Mary's attachment patterns reinforced the lack of safety and security in their marriage. Each partner's coping behavior drove the other into a more rigid presentation of *their* coping behavior. Mary pursued Jim for reassurance, so Jim withdrew to seek calm—which only caused Mary to pursue him even more. Learning about their attachment patterns helped them work toward a securely attached marriage. Mary softened her approach to Jim, and Jim practiced staying engaged.

Another couple I worked with, Jack and Susan, came together quickly when Jack pursued Susan. Jack was affectionate and passionate in wooing Susan, seeking a physical connection, and showering her with affirmations. At the same time, he sought her affection and affirmation. When they had their first child and Susan's focus was distracted, Jack became sullen and distant. Things would improve when they were able to schedule a getaway, but in their day-to- day life, Jack kept pulling away. Shortly after their second child was born, Susan discovered that he was having an emotional affair. She was blindsided because he hadn't talked to her about his dissatisfaction in their relationship.

"I just thought we were going through what most couples go through with the stressors of starting a family," Susan told me. "We still spent time together. He never talked about his emotions with me."

Jack had a disorganized attachment pattern. He sometimes pursued Susan when he felt like her love was focused on the children; at other times, he sabotaged the relationship by turning to the affection and attention of another woman. In their interactions, he alternated between outbursts of anger, neediness, overt expressions of love, and complete inattention.

Working with disorganized attached people is challenging because there isn't a consistent coping strategy. It takes time and effort to map the cycle of interactions and work toward a more secure attachment. Fortunately, Jack and Susan were committed to doing the work; with time and practice they began to understand each other's needs.

Protest Systems

Emotional withdrawal, the silent treatment, and arguing are behaviors that partners resort to when they're discontented, frustrated, dissatisfied, or unfulfilled in their relationships.

These protest behaviors often stem from unmet needs, unexpressed emotions, or a sense of powerlessness. Protests are necessary ways in which people communicate their dissatisfaction, in hopes of initiating change or gaining attention from their partner. Unhealthy protest systems, however, are detrimental to a marriage if they're not addressed, because they create a cycle of negative interactions and erode the intimate bond between partners.

Recognizing and understanding protest systems is a crucial step in resolving a couple's underlying issues and rebuilding their relationship. The following chart shows healthy and unhealthy protest cycles for the anxious and avoidant attachment patterns.

	Anxious Attachment	*Dismissive/Avoidant Attachment*
	Pursuer ⟶	Withdrawer ⟶
Unhealthy Fight Cycle	Criticism Anger Accusations Labeling Overplanning Anxiousness Excessive talking	Avoiding Shutting down Staying busy Distracted Leaving Overworking Silence
Healthy Protest Cycle	Soften tone and voice volume Reach vulnerability with "I" statements Use primary emotions and congruent behavioral body language Accept comfort and reassurance	Stay engaged emotionally and verbally Develop stress tolerance skills Use validation and empathic responses to help de-escalate emotions Speak needs for safety

Unhealthy Protest Systems

Jim and Mary are an example of how an unhealthy protest system plays out with an anxious partner (Mary) and an avoidant partner (Jim).

When Jim came home late, Mary was angry and criticized him harshly. She accused him of not caring about their family. She made elaborate nightly dinners, and while they ate, she talked and talked. She constantly pursued Jim, seeking comfort and reassurance.

Mary's protest behaviors caused Jim to withdraw. In order to feel safe, Jim needed space. To avoid Mary's pursuit at home, Jim took on more responsibility at work, and when he was home, he found ways to keep busy. Jim's protests made Mary more anxious and caused her to pursue Jim even more.

Eventually, Jim and Mary avoided any challenging conversations, and they stopped spending much time together. Their communication shut down on nearly all levels. They even moved into separate rooms.

Healthy Protest Systems

To move from an anxious attachment pattern to secure attachment, Mary had to practice softening her tone and lowering her voice. She learned to use "I" statements instead of "you" statements so she didn't come across as accusatory. She changed her nonverbal communication, too—no more eye rolling or disgusted facial expressions.

Jim practiced staying present and engaged in their conversations and worked on stress tolerance techniques. He learned to use validation and empathic responses to help Mary de- escalate when she was anxious, and he forced himself to speak up about his emotional needs instead of simply withdrawing.

Healthy protest systems allow couples to move toward their partner when the other is protesting. They are able to provide emotional regulation while the other is able to receive comfort and reassurance allowing them to stop fighting against each other and start fighting for each other.

If the underlying processes in a relationship are rooted in insecure attachment, couples can't develop intimacy or work through disagreements. Over time, romantic emotions, desire, passion, and companionship fade away, and they act out of duty and obligation.

Jim and Mary realized many factors impacted their marriage. Some of their triggers stemmed from their family histories. As they worked toward secure attachment, Jim opened up to Mary, which helped her understand him better. Jim also shifted his viewpoint to see Mary through more loving eyes. Mary realized she'd been telling herself a story about Jim that wasn't true.

They also connected with the brain science part of my intensive. Jim realized that when he's upset, his back brain takes over, causing him to be unreasonable and unable to hear Mary. Now, he and Mary have learned how to help each other shift from the back brain to the front brain. That was a game-changer.

Today, after going through the intensive, spending time in prayer, and using tools I gave them, Jim and Mary are a team again. Even their spiritual health has changed drastically, and they're on a really good path.

The attachment process is biologically hardwired into the brain for our protection in infancy and childhood. Understanding attachment patterns helps us see our partner's behaviors differently.

God, in his creative wisdom, designed our brain through the attachment system of His plan. It ensures protection of connection, physical and emotional regulation with a significant other. It is so important to our survival; it is not good for man to be alone.

The neuroscience understanding of romantic love and attachment better illustrates this.

CHAPTER REFLECTION

 We are hardwired to protect ourselves from emotional threats by co-regulating with a caregiver in childhood and persists in a romantic partnership in adulthood, both necessary to protect your most important relationships throughout the span of life. Because of your intimate, co-regulating relationship, your spouse can present an emotional threat more easily than anyone else.

Identifying what you and your spouse's tendencies of fight, flight, or freeze in protest moments is helpful. Attachment patterns provide a framework to help us understand the biological drive for our behaviors.

CHAPTER 4:

Proper Protest Systems: Managing Conflict

. . . .

When I was a child, I talked like a child, I thought like a child,
I reasoned like a child. When I became a man,
I put the ways of childhood behind me. . .
Now I know in part; then I shall know fully,
even as I am fully known.
1 Corinthians 13:11-12

In a marriage, a proper protest system is a healthy and constructive way for partners to express their concerns, needs, or dissatisfaction. Proper protest systems allow open communication. They enable partners to voice their feelings without resorting to harmful or destructive behaviors.

Proper protest systems are needed . . .
- So, couples can know each other deeply.
- To restore connection when there is a disagreement.
- To reduce the stressors of life.

Protest systems equip couples to tackle problems as a team with practices such as . . .

- Expressing concerns in a clear and nonconfrontational way.
- Listening to each other's perspectives.
- Showing empathy and understanding.
- Respecting each other's viewpoints.
- Avoiding dismissive or contemptuous behavior.
- Working collaboratively toward solutions and compromises.
- Seeking outside help when it's needed.

Natalia and Gary's marriage was disconnected and broken. Instead of communicating and resolving conflicts, they were pointing fingers at each other. Gary had left home for a period of time, and Natalia wasn't even sure if he was committed to working on their marriage. They were desperate for wise, biblical counsel, but things were so bad that they weren't sure they could wait the three weeks until my next open intensive.

> **Conflict is a *normal* part of married life. It is *impossible* for two people to agree on *everything***

There are moments of dissatisfaction and unmet needs in every relationship. A healthy protest system is a set of behaviors that enable you to safely express and work through your concerns, ultimately strengthening the bond with your partner. Embracing a healthy protest system is the key to unlocking healthy communication, conflict resolution, and overall well-being in your marriage.

Managing Stress with Protest Systems

Life is full of stressors, internal and external (see the chart below). Internal stressors include things like relationship dynamics; external stressors are pressures that come from the circumstances of life. When you and your partner have a disagreement, it's important to recognize that you both are under internal and external stressors.

If a couple is embroiled in a fight cycle, it's hard for them to manage life's stressors. One partner's protest—perhaps a complaint about the division of labor in the household—causes a back-brain response from the other, which leads to an argument and leaves the original issue unresolved. As unresolved conflicts pile up, they become more and more problematic to the relationship. Natalia and Gary didn't have a healthy protest system, so when they were pressed by the normal stresses of life, their relationship crumbled.

If a couple has a healthy protest system, they're better equipped to handle life's stressors. They practice overriding the primitive, back-brain response to conflict. They converse with each other with curiosity, opening to understand one another. A protest from one or the other leads to resolution of the conflict and reconnection in the relationship. It allows for reconnection of both parties to their front brain in order to access problem-solving.

Internal vs. *External* Stressors

Internal Stressors	*External Stressors*
• internal pressures pushing against	• outside pressures pushing in
• division of labor in the home	• workload pressures
• parenting idealogy	• parenting demands and challenges
• financial ideology differences	• extended family demands, traditions, expectations
• desires for intimate connection emotionally, physically, and sexually	• financial demands and challenges
• lack of mutually shared interests, hobbies, goals, dreams	• time/schedule constraints for connection
• differences in spiritual, religious practice, or value sets	• life challenges preventing goals, dreams, interests, hobbies
	• work/life balance

Emotional Flooding

When we're under stress, we're more emotional; we become *emotionally flooded*.

Being emotionally flooded refers to a state of intense emotional overwhelm in which our thoughts, feelings, and reactions are significantly heightened. Emotional flooding occurs when our emotional response to a situation exceeds our capacity to effectively process or manage our emotions. In this state, our back brain takes over and we either fight, flee, or freeze. I use the terms *fighter*, *flighter*, and *freezer* to refer to people by their habitual response to emotional flooding.

When we're emotionally flooded . . .

- Rational thinking and problem-solving abilities are compromised.
- The surge of intense emotions we feel—such as anger, fear, sadness, or frustration—may lead to impulsive or irrational behavior.
- We have difficulty communicating effectively, listening attentively, or engaging in constructive conflict resolution.

External emotional flooding results in behaviors like crying, yelling, harsh or rapid speech, criticism, or increased activity. These behaviors are common in arguments.

Internal emotional flooding results in difficulty with concentration and being slow to respond in conversation. This is more common in individuals who tend to flee or freeze in conflicts. They may appear emotionally blank. Consequently, others often underestimate their level of emotional distress.

However, it is crucial to recognize that everyone who experiences emotional flooding—external or internal—is equally distressed, no matter how they look on the outside. Whether our response to conflict is to fight, flee, or freeze, our back brain takes over when we're emotionally flooded, impairing rational thinking. Couples need to acknowledge the effects of emotional

> The *fighter* has an *external* presentation and the *freezer/flighter* has an *internal* presentation, each equally emotionally flooded

flooding and empathize with each other. When we support our partners during emotional flooding, we foster more compassionate and resilient relationships.

Whether we fight, flee, or freeze when we're emotionally flooded, the overarching factor is that we're in autopilot, governed by our back brain. A fighter's face won't look the same as an anxious flighter's face, but the same thing is happening in the brain.

Fight Cycles

When a couple gets stuck in a fight cycle, they can't work through important issues. Gradually, this erodes their emotional bond of safety and security.

Proper protest systems enable couples to address issues and find agreement, seek reassurance, and reconnect. Without a proper protest system, disconnection mounts and reduces the sense of safety and security in a relationship.

In unhealthy fight cycles, protests are counterproductive. Instead of resulting in care, comfort, and reconnection, protests initiate fights. If couples are unable to manage life's stressors or relationship challenges, the stressors and challenges simply compound. Wounds don't heal because the broken protest system doesn't leave room for healing conversations. Positive sentiment declines, intimacy fades, and safety and security vanish. As mentioned in Chapter 1, it is the greatest predictor of divorce. It's that important.

Fight Cycle

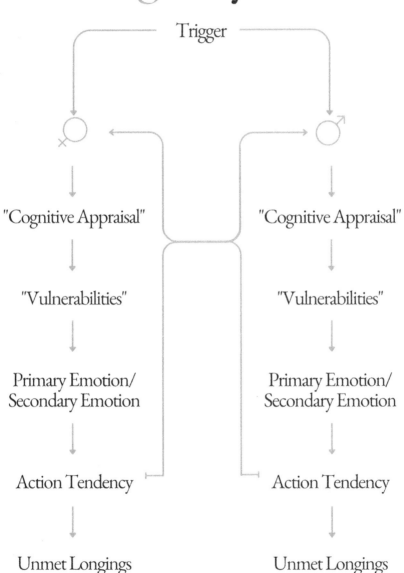

Trigger

"Cognitive Appraisal"

"Vulnerabilities"

Primary Emotion/
Secondary Emotion

Action Tendency

Unmet Longings

"Cognitive Appraisal"

"Vulnerabilities"

Primary Emotion/
Secondary Emotion

Action Tendency

Unmet Longings

Gary and Natalia's fight cycle was ingrained in their relationship. One major conflict resulted when Gary decided to take out a loan to help his mother without consulting Natalia. Not only did this leave Natalia feeling angry and ignored; it also strained their finances.

Other conflicts revolved around trivial incidents. For example, one day Natalia forgot to buy a ham Gary had requested for a family gathering. He accused her of being selfish and insensitive, and the incident escalated into a full-blown argument. But the fight wasn't really about the ham.

The underlying issue was the disconnect in their relationship, which stemmed from a lack of open communication and shared decision making—exemplified by Gary unilaterally taking out the loan. The ham incident was a trigger that highlighted deeper unresolved issues in their relationship.

Gary had an annual work convention, and that year it was going to be in Paris. Natalia was looking forward to going with Gary. She thought the time together in a romantic city might help them reconnect. But Gary had been asked to give a presentation in front of the entire organization and needed to be able to focus and have peace. Bringing Natalia along wasn't an option. When Gary told Natalia she couldn't come, she was hurt, and then angry. How dare Gary not include her?

That's when Natalia and Gary came to see me. They had been in marriage counseling for years and wondered if my advice would be any different from what they'd heard before.

Primary and Secondary Emotions

As Natalia and Gary embarked on their journey of self-discovery, seeking to understand the intricate workings of their relationship, I introduced them to the concept of primary and secondary emotions, which shed light on the hidden layers beneath their interactions.

Our hardwired, biologically based threat systems generate protests. These protests often take the form of emotions that signal unmet needs. When Natalia and Gary expressed frustration, annoyance, or discontent to each other, they weren't just attacking each other—although that's how they typically perceived those things. Rather, their expressions of discontent were bids for connection, comfort, or reassurance.

When we have conflict in our relationships, we experience two types of emotions: primary and secondary.

Primary emotions are the first emotions you feel in any given situation. They're usually softer emotions—feelings of sadness, hurt, rejection, or abandonment. For example, Natalia was hurt when Gary excluded her from his annual work convention.

Secondary emotions are what you feel after primary emotions. They're usually more intense emotions that protect us or push people away. For example, after being hurt when Gary excluded her from his convention, Natalia felt indignant and angry.

In a marriage with a healthy protest system, a partner can make a *vulnerable reach*—they can express their deepest emotions, needs, and concerns to their partner in a genuine and open way. In a vulnerable reach, you're emotionally exposed, often uncomfortable, and risk rejection. Making a vulnerable reach requires emotional transparency and trust that your partner will receive and respond to your opening with empathy, understanding, and support.

Natalia and Gary started to see how primary emotions— like Natalia's sadness about the trip to Paris—were opportunities for vulnerable reaches. If they had a healthy protest system in place, Natalia could have expressed her sadness, Gary could have responded with understanding, and Natalia would never have shifted into the secondary emotion of anger.

Protest Systems and the Attachment Process

Dr. Edward Tronick, Director of the Child Development Unit at the University of Massachusetts Boston, carried out a study known as "The Still Face Experiment" in 1975. [1] The experiment was based on the observation that when an infant experiences emotional stress—for instance, if they feel unsafe or rejected due to a lack of response from their caregiver—they respond with signs of distress and discomfort.

Dr. Tronick had mothers interact with their babies while displaying either positive or neutral facial expressions. Keeping the caregiver in close proximity, emotionally and physically, is one of a baby's natural survival skills. Tronick found that when a mother maintained a neutral facial expression, her child would try a succession of approaches to induce the mother to reconnect emotionally and physically—perhaps smiling, pointing, reaching, screeching, turning away, and crying. With each unsuccessful attempt to reconnect, the baby's emotional distress would increase. However, as soon as the mother responded, the baby's emotions were soothed.

When we share things with our partners, we watch their response, just like a baby watches their mother's face. When you and your partner exchange information about each other, you get to know each other better and build more intimacy. It's easy to share positive emotions or things you like; it's much harder to tell your partner that you don't like something they're doing. Talking about what's bothering us brings up differences of culture, opinion, perspective, preference, habit, and personality—and so on. There are differences in experience, gender differences, differences in family of origin, ethics, and traditions.

We need to have the means to reveal these things to our partner so we can know each other. When we share something that's bothering us, we watch how our partner responds, because it matters to us if our partner sees us in a non-benevolent way. It's easy to feel threatened if they respond in a negative way. But if we learn to manage the way we see their response, we can also manage whether we feel threatened by it or not. The same is true when our partner comes to us with something that's bothering them.

Conflict triggers the brain's primitive response to fight, flee, or freeze.

If you see a conflict—your partner's protest—as a threat, you start telling yourself a story in your head. *My partner is not loving, accepting, or responsive.* This activates your body's threat system: fight, flee, or freeze. You feel it viscerally, in your stomach or chest. You naturally begin a protest of your own.

The problem is when either protest is so harsh that it works *against* the goal of reconnecting. A harsh protest looks different depending on whether you're a fighter, flighter, or freezer. For a fighter, it might be harsh words; for a flighter, a retreat to another room; and for a freezer, it might be a blank stare.

Unhealthy protest systems or fight cycles involve interaction governed by the reactionary, self- protective back brain. Remember, when we're in the back brain, we're not accessing the higher- order emotional and reasoning skills housed in our front brain: problem solving, conflict management, empathy, and stress tolerance.

In a back brain–dominated conflict, you may do and say unreasonable things or violate your own morals, ethics, and spiritual principles. You have no empathy toward your spouse because your own distress blocks your ability to perceive that your partner is in distress. After such a conflict, you may regret your conduct or something you said. When conflict is consistently intense over an

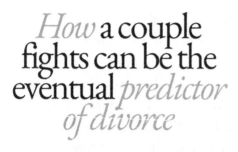
How a couple fights can be the eventual *predictor of divorce*

extended period of time, it becomes habitual and impacts our sleeping and eating patterns. For example, when Natalia and Gary were stuck in a rigid fight cycle, she started having a glass of wine every night to help turn off her racing mind and get to sleep.

Fighting Styles Can Predict Divorce: Gottman's Four Horsemen

Dr. John Gottman,[2] a world-renowned marriage expert, has conducted 40 years of longitudinal studies on couples. He can predict with over 90% accuracy which marriages will end in divorce based on just four aspects of unhealthy protest systems. He dubbed these four behaviors the "Four Horsemen of the Apocalypse."[3] If they're not corrected, they're extremely detrimental to relationships.

The First Horseman: Defensiveness

The first horseman is defensiveness. Suppose a wife comes to her husband with a complaint—something he does that she doesn't like. Her husband responds to her complaint by defending his behavior. Defensiveness can include denying responsibility, making excuses, or counterattacking. It is the inability to receive your partner's influence or feedback.

For example, a defensive partner might . . .

- Respond to a complaint by saying, "It's not my fault. You're just too sensitive!"

- Shift blame onto their partner by saying, "If you hadn't done _____, I wouldn't have reacted this way!"
- Bringing up their partner's past mistakes to deflect from the current issue.

The Second Horseman: Criticism

The second horseman is criticism. A husband may have a hard time receiving his wife's protest because of the way it's presented—it comes across as a personal attack, not a discussion about a behavior or a specific issue. Criticism includes labeling, name-calling, and attacking someone's character or personality; it is attacking the person, not the problem. If a protest is presented in a hurtful way, it's hard to receive graciously.

For example, a critical partner might say . . .

- "You never listen to me. You're so self-absorbed!"
- "You're always late. You're so irresponsible!"
- "You're such a slob. You never clean up after yourself!"
- "You're a sorry excuse for a father."
- "You are the epitome of what the Bible calls a nagging wife."

The Third Horseman: Stonewalling

The third horseman is stonewalling. A stonewaller responds to conflict by withdrawing, shutting down and refusing to engage in discussion. Rather than actively trying to work things out, they take a passive-aggressive or punitive approach. Stonewalling usually stems from someone being unable to regulate themselves enough to have difficult conversations and problem solve.

For example, a stonewalling partner might . . .

- Give their partner the silent treatment, ignoring the other party's attempts to communicate or resolve an issue.
- Physically leave the room or withdraw emotionally.

- Disengage by appearing disinterested, not making eye contact, or not responding.

The Fourth Horseman: Contempt

The fourth horseman is contempt. Contempt is a general disregard for someone or something. In a marriage, contempt is a toxic mix of resentment, disgust, and superiority toward a partner, often expressed in insults, mockery, or belittling. A contemptuous partner doesn't care that their partner is in distress; they don't have any desire to restore peace and harmony.

For example, a contemptuous partner might . . .

- Roll their eyes or use sarcasm when their partner shares thoughts or feelings.
- Mock their partner's interests or hobbies, making them feel insignificant.
- Call their partner names or insult them.

Dr. Gottman says that, of the four horsemen, contempt is the strongest sign that a couple is headed toward divorce; it's the hardest one to recover from. I don't disagree, but I believe there's one additional factor that nearly as difficult to overcome.

Another Relationship Killer: Indifference

In my experience working with couples, indifference is another strong predictor of divorce. When a partner is indifferent toward their marriage, they've reached the point of not caring about it—like someone who's contemptuous. But with indifference, there aren't any contemptuous insults; there's simply no emotion at all. An indifferent partner has shut down; what happens to the relationship doesn't matter to them anymore.

Indifference includes a lack of interest, concern, or emotional investment in a relationship. It's characterized by detachment, apathy, or disengagement. Indifference may show up in a marriage as unwillingness to address issues or work toward improvement.

For example, an indifferent partner might say . . .

- "I don't care anymore. It's not worth putting in the effort."
- "Why bother? Nothing's going to change."
- "I'm not interested in what you have to say. It's not my problem."
- "We're just going through the motions."
- "I have better things to do than work on this relationship."
- "Your feelings don't matter to me. Deal with it yourself."

It's important to address and work through indifference in a marriage, because it creates a significant barrier to emotional connection, satisfaction, and overall relationship well-being. Open, honest communication, seeking professional help, and a willingness to actively invest in the relationship can all help overcome indifference and foster a more fulfilling and connected marriage.

Recognizing Disconnect Cycles

Gary and Natalia's fight cycle changed their internal narratives about each other. The incident with the ham was part of a larger story, one that involved deep-seated emotions tied to their family backgrounds and past relationship experiences.

If the stories we're telling ourselves about are partners are negative, virtually anything—even a forgotten ham—can be perceived as a threat and activate our instinctive back-brain warning system. When that happens, we immediately shift from vulnerable primary emotions like sadness and hurt to self-protective secondary emotions like anger and indifference. Secondary emotions fuel our habitual threat response: fight, flee, or freeze.

Gary and Natalia's fight cycle was driven by a combination of unexpressed primary emotions and self-protective secondary emotions. Gary and Natalia came to me for help in breaking free from this damaging pattern. They wanted to rewrite their story, foster understanding, and empathy, and develop healthy ways of addressing their emotions and needs.

Example of Mapped
Disconnect **Cycle**

Coming Home Late
From Work

"He is never home when he says he will be. He doesn't appreciate my contribution of preparing a meal for us. Everything else is more important."

"She doesn't understand the pressures I feel at work. I'm not in control of how long meetings go. I'm working hard to provide for us."

"I'm unimportant."

"I'm not appreciated or understood."

Lonely, Sad, Hurt
Angry

Hurt, Disrespected
Indifference

Complain
Accuse
Attack
Passive Aggressive Actions

Shut down
Withdraw
Withold Communication
Cold Body Language

Desire to Connect

Desire to have a soft place to fall

As I worked with them, Gary and Natalia began to understand their disconnect cycle. The disconnect cycle is hardwired into us for our self-defense, but if it happens often enough to become chronic, the hardwired, back-brain neural pathways become rigid and activate more and more quickly. Gary and Natalia were stuck in a chronic fight cycle; we needed to override the system and create new neural pathways so they could interact in a healthy way.

Once neural pathways form in the brain, they can't be destroyed. However, brain research shows that the brain is *neuroplastic*—that is, the brain can form *new* neural pathways that go around the old ones. In other words, although Gary and Natalia had forged neural pathways that reinforced their chronic fight cycle, they could develop new pathways that promote healthy, safe protests and productive reconnection responses.

In our two-day intensive and a follow-up program, Gary and Natalia hunkered down and worked through issues they had avoided for years. They practiced working through their disconnect cycle together, reaching through prickly protests to catch each other with empathy and understanding.

Today, their marriage is the healthiest it's ever been. They've learned to express frustration without blaming each other. They connect with grace and understanding, and they pause and assess situations before jumping to conclusions. Life is still busy, but they're working as a team, not against each other. In the past, they've had issues with Gary's mom; now, they use the same principles that helped restore their marriage when they interact with her. Consequently, Gary's mom feels heard and understood.

It's difficult to break out of a toxic, chronic fight cycle without outside help. But with the proper assistance, it's possible—just look at Gary and Natalia. They were able to begin seeing protests from a different perspective.

I've created a form to help you map your disconnect cycle. You can download it from:
www.nakedandexposedbook.com/resources.

CHAPTER REFLECTION

Using the Disconnect Cycle Form, map your most recent disconnect cycle so you and your partner can understand it better. Enter into the assignment with a curious attitude to gain understanding.

CHAPTER 5:

Perceiving Protests: Learning to Receive Another Viewpoint

. . . .

Instead, speaking the truth in love, we will grow
to become in every respect the mature body of him
who is the head, that is, Christ.

EPHESIANS 4:15

The first step toward restoring intimacy in your marriage is to learn to understand your partner and reframe your perception of their protests.

After ten years of marriage, Robert and Rebecca were stuck in a destructive fight cycle that kept them alternately arguing and not speaking to each other. Actually, this cycle had run throughout their entire marriage; to their reckoning, their marriage had never been healthy. Rebecca felt rejected, alone, and hopeless. Robert felt unloved, unsupported, and helpless. Although they had spent quite a bit of money on counseling, they were considering divorce.

As a last-ditch attempt to save their marriage, they came to see me. Robert was skeptical. Traditional counseling hadn't done much for them. They would get some help on current issues, but never solved any of their core problems. So, they kept repeating the same cycle. Robert was a flighter; Rebecca was a fighter. When they clashed, Robert withdrew, and Rebecca escalated and pursued him, pushing him to flee even more.

Protests: A Normal and Necessary Part of a Relationship

When an infant fusses, his mother doesn't say, "This kid's never happy!" She tries to understand what he needs—milk, a diaper change, or a nap—and then meet the need.

The baby can't feed himself; he needs help from his mother. His protest—fussing and crying—are normal and necessary because they remind her to feed him.

Although our protests are very different from a baby's fussing, they're still a normal and necessary part of our relationships. The problem in many marriages is that spouses respond to one another's protests as if they're a mother saying, "This kid's never happy!"—except it sounds like:

- "He's never happy with me."
- "She's such a nag."

A protest is an opportunity for a couple to restore their connection. The challenge is to change the way we see protests:

- "He's revealing things he wants me to know and understand, and it matters to me."
- "She's telling me what she needs and how she wants to deepen our connection."

Changing your interpretation of a moment of protest enables you to respond in a way that doesn't threaten your partner. Instead of interacting with them in back-brain fight-flight-or-freeze mode, you can listen with curiosity and empathy. You can avoid falling back on a rigid, negative narrative and change the story you're telling yourself about them to something more benevolent.

To develop intimacy, you need to understand how your partner is hardwired, what triggers them, and what their sensitivities and vulnerabilities are. When you and your partner are aware of each other's vulnerabilities, you can cultivate a culture of care in your relationship—far different from the rigidity evident in so many fight cycles: "He is so _____" and "She is so _____."

Robert and Rebecca came into counseling expecting me to referee their disagreements.

"I just need a third person in the room to make him understand how his views and behaviors are wrong," Rebecca told me. "I need someone to validate me."

"I don't think Rebecca sees or remembers things accurately. I really feel like we are in two totally different realms of reality," Robert said. "I need someone to be a witness and point out who's right."

They had recently had their biggest fight ever. Robert went on a long business trip, but only checked in once a day, late at night—often well after Rebecca had gone to bed. When he came home, she threatened him with divorce. One of the first things they wanted me to do was to make arrangements for Robert's communication when he was traveling for business: when he would call and how long they would talk.

Robert and Rebecca were fighting about nearly *everything* without any kind of resolution. They saw things in opposite ways.

Intervening as a referee wouldn't have helped them because of one simple reason:

Perceptual truth is real to the individual in the moment. Absolute truth is known only to God.

If I acted merely as a referee, I might settle some disputes by taking one side or the other or declaring some compromises. But that wouldn't change the fact that they each believed only their own perception of each disagreement.

When you disagree with your partner, you say, "I see this." Your partner says, "Well, I see that."

Each of you is fully convinced that the way you're seeing things is the entire picture, the only way the situation needs to be seen. You're not thinking about:

- Gender differences
- Your different life experiences
- Your varied gifts, talents, and personalities
- Your genetic differences

All these factors influence the way we make sense of the world.

When Rebecca and Robert met, she was attracted to his outgoing personality and sense of humor; he always carried the conversation in social settings. Rebecca was an introvert, and Robert made her feel at ease. Robert admired Rebecca's attention to detail, organizational skills, and ability to multitask. Early in their marriage, she was working, furthering her education, volunteering at church, and managing their kids and home like clockwork.

But when they disagreed, each of them wanted the idiosyncrasies that once attracted them to each other to disappear. Robert wanted Rebecca to think and act like him. Rebecca wanted Robert to think and act like her.

They needed a new perspective—the perspective of an investigator at a crime scene.

Perceiving Protests: Crime Scene Investigation

Imagine you're investigating a crime, and you've learned that there were two eyewitnesses.

Naturally, you would interview both witnesses, recognizing that each saw the event from a different angle and can provide a unique perspective that helps you reconstruct what happened. By combining their reports, you gain a more comprehensive and accurate summary of the truth.

Similarly, couples with healthy protest systems don't rely only on their own version of events. When they have disagreements, they explore each other's viewpoints. Each is open to hearing their partner's perspective, understanding that it adds valuable insight and rounds out the overall picture of the situation.

Your partner may say, "From my angle, I see A, B, and C, which leads me to conclude D." You add this information to your perception of the truth.

Then, your partner comes over to your side of the crime scene; that is, you share your perspective—what you see and how you're making sense of the situation.

You're not stuck with just *his* angle and *her* angle—you have an *us* angle.

Remember, all either of you have is *perceptual* truth, what's real to you in the moment. Because of this, your two perspectives are complementary. Putting them together allows you to move forward together with a full version of the truth, an 'us' truth.

When you're open to adding to the story you're telling yourself about a conflict with your partner, you can shift your view of the situation to something much less threatening, which, in turn, can settle your secondary emotions and soften your prickly protest behaviors. Put another way, receiving your partner's perspective can soothe your reactionary back brain and allow your rational prefrontal cortex to come back online. Then you can solve problems together as a team, an 'us' team.

When partners are grounded in the front brain, they appreciate and embrace each other's unique qualities and quirks. Those idiosyncrasies are merely sticks on the path. However, in moments of protest, they see each other in a less favorable light, and those same idiosyncrasies are like snakes on the path. The back brain is active, processing what it sees as a threat.

We dislike the idea of the person we care about most perceiving us negatively. We resist hearing them present an unflattering picture of us. Hence, we enter self-defense mode, attempting to convince our partner that their perception is flawed—they saw a stick, not a snake.

It's challenging to accept that our loved one is upset with us. We instinctively perceive this as a threat and resort to self-protection, trying to invalidate their evidence. This response is the back brain activating, and it's what makes it difficult to interrupt a rigid fight cycle. We're afraid that if we accept our partner's truth, it will become our truth.

However, we're talking about *perceptual* truth. When we acknowledge our partner's perceptual truth, we're *adding* to our truth. Hearing their perspective and making sense of it doesn't mean we're blindly accepting their version of events as our own. Rather, we're taking the opportunity to gain a more comprehensive understanding of the truth as a whole.

In a healthy protest system, couples don't look at each other as enemies; they each receive the other's version of what happened in a conflict. In a healthy protest system, the fight cycle is the enemy, not your partner. Rather than battling each other, you're tackling the problem—together.

When your partner protests something and your back brain perceives it as a threat, you override the fight, flight, or freeze response, knowing that the real threat isn't your partner—the real threat is the disconnect cycle.

In healthy protest systems, you enter a conflict situation holding your truth *loosely*. You know that the story you're telling yourself is merely your own perceptual truth. You're open to comparing your truth with your partner's truth. You share with each other, in a soft way, the things that are bothering you, using language like:

- "Right now, I'm feeling like . . ."
- "What I'm thinking right now is . . ."
- "The story I'm telling myself is…"

Couples with healthy protest systems use one other to regulate stress. A wife is stressed or upset. She reaches out in a soft, healthy way, and her husband moves toward her. Immediately, her stress hormones start to decrease. They're using each other to regulate their stress and emotions. When couples approach disagreements with an open mind rather than holding to the rigid stories in their head, they can use each other's feedback to settle the emotional trigger, rewrite the internal narrative, and return to an '*us*' dynamic.

Healthy Couples **seek to understand** *each other* **rather than seeking to be** *understood*

Connect Cycle

♀   ♂

Trigger

Cognitive Appraisal
"The story I'm telling
myself."

↓

Vulnerabilities/
Sensitivies/
Attachment Wounds

↓

(Primary Emotion)

↓

Soft Protest
Share from place of
vulnerability use of
primary emotion

"Catch Method"
Validate
Empathic Response
Soft Touch
Curious Questions
Room to Share
Repair Reassure

↓

Other side of the
crime scene:

♂ Share
♀ Catch

↓

Met Longings

In unhealthy argument cycles, each partner rejects the other's version of a conflict situation. There's no crime scene investigation, and instead of a broad summary report, they each have only their own narrow perceptual truth.

Healthy Protest Case Study: Sarah and Mark

Let's use an imaginary couple, Sarah and Mark, to illustrate the dynamics of a healthy protest system and the importance of understanding each other's perspectives.

One evening, Sarah reaches out to Mark to express her appreciation for the time they're spending together.

"Honey, I'm really enjoying this evening," Sarah says. "Thank you for making this time for us. I love being with you."

"Yeah," Mark replies. Sarah wonders if he's fully present or even listening to her.

She immediately begins to create a story in her head. *Is he acting this way because he finds me unattractive or boring? Maybe he didn't really hear me.* She decides to give it another try.

"Hey, maybe you didn't hear me earlier. I just wanted you to know how much I appreciate you and enjoy being with you. You're my best friend, and I can't imagine being anywhere else but with you."

Once again, Mark just says, "Yeah." He doesn't even look at Sarah. The story in Sarah's head is solidifying. She's pretty sure that Mark is no longer interested in her. She feels hurt and neglected.

But Sarah gathers the courage to make a healthy protest.

"Honey, I'm trying to connect with you, but I feel unimportant, like you're brushing me off and not even looking at me. The story I'm telling myself is that you don't find me interesting anymore."

Mark doesn't get defensive or dismissive; instead, he responds empathetically, trying to understand Sarah's perspective.

"I don't understand. Can you explain what you're talking about?"

"Well, I told you twice how much I appreciate you and enjoy spending time with you, and it seemed like you were just blowing me off," Sarah tells him. "You didn't even make eye contact."

Mark acknowledges her experience. "I see how you could interpret it that way," he says. "From your side, it may have seemed like I was dismissing you."

Mark has gained credibility with Sarah by acknowledging her feelings. Now, he shares his own side of the story.

"I just got off the phone with my boss a little while ago, and I'm having a hard time. I didn't really hear what you said because I was trying to ward off a panic attack."

Sarah is willing to consider Mark's perspective and incorporate it into her understanding of the situation, and this allows them to establish a deeper connection. Sarah realizes that Mark's response had nothing to do with a lack of interest in her; it resulted from his own emotional struggle. They recognize that it was a difficult moment for both of them and discuss how they can handle similar situations differently in the future. In doing so, they foster a deeper understanding and connection, building a stronger foundation for their relationship.

In this example of a healthy protest system, Sarah and Mark:

- Shifted their focus from personal insecurities and misunderstandings to a collaborative approach.
- Moved away from thoughts like, "He thinks I'm not interesting," and "I can't share my struggles with her."
- Viewed the issue as something that affected both of them instead of blaming each other.

- Asked, "What can we do together to handle this situation differently in the future?"

When they reframed their internal narratives, a potentially negative situation became an opportunity to seek beneficial solutions for their relationship as a whole. They prioritized their partnership, understanding that working together is crucial for growth and connection.

This is the very process of growing new neural pathways, reducing areas of insecurities and helping one another grow more in emotional intelligence by enhancing stress tolerance and positive coping skills.

Perceiving Protests: Like Parent to Child

You can trace the protest system you see in your marriage back to your relationship with your parents.

Imagine a child playing on a playground, occasionally glancing back to check if Mom is still watching them play. If the child makes eye contact and sees Mom smiling, they're reassured and continue playing and exploring. However, if the child looks back and Mom isn't there, playtime comes to a screeching halt. The child's threat-response system activates, initiating fight, flight, or freeze behaviors. For example, the child may:

- Call out, "Mommy!"
- Frantically search for Mom.
- Stand in place, crying, until Mom comes to reassure them.

These behaviors are the child's protests. The goal of the protests is to alleviate distress and regain connection with Mom. Once their connection is reestablished and the child's emotions are regulated, the tears subside, the smile returns, and they resume playing.

As this process is repeated, the child becomes more secure, feels supported, and freely explores their surroundings.

The dynamics between marital partners mirror the parent–child protest system.

Just as the child looks back to ensure a parent's presence and support, we have moments of uncertainty in our relationships when we need reassurance from our partner. If our partner's reassurance is lacking, we may initiate a protest, expressing our distress in some way. When we reconnect and our emotional needs are met, we feel secure and continue navigating life together.

Protest systems play a vital role in maintaining and strengthening the bond between partners in a relationship, providing safety, support, and freedom to explore and grow together.

Here's another illustration. Imagine you've taught your son how to ride a bike. A big part of your instruction is, "Never ride your bike without a helmet."

However, one day he forgets his helmet. He's having so much fun riding his bike that he goes faster than he can handle. He loses control, falls, and comes running into the house.

"Mommy, Daddy, I crashed!" He's crying, his knees and elbows are scraped, and there's a big goose egg on his head.

The goose egg is a clear indication that he wasn't wearing his helmet. But what's your first response?

You scoop him up and sit him at the kitchen table. You wash off his knees and elbows and put a bag of frozen peas on the lump on his head.

Once the flood of tears has ebbed, the scrapes are bandaged, and everything is calm, you ask,

"So where was your helmet?"

You respond first with compassion and care. Your care de-escalates the situation. Then you're able to have a calm, rational conversation about the helmet. Responding with compassion first develops a culture of care within a relationship.

The Catch Method

The Catch Method is a way of responding to your partner when they are protesting.

I developed the Catch Method based on my years of experience in counseling couples. Properly applied, it nurtures a culture of care in a marriage and helps maintain appropriate protests and a healthy fight cycle.

When your spouse is in some form of distress and reaches out to you, they want you to be there for them. They want to know that what they're going through matters to you. When they reach out to you, it's like they're stepping off the edge of a cliff, hoping you'll be there to catch them.

If you and your spouse learn to use the Catch Method, you'll be agents of de-escalation in moments of conflict, helping each other shift from back brain to front brain so you can engage in rational and intentional conversation and solve problems together.

Let's illustrate with the story about Robert's work convention in Paris.

Robert wanted Rebecca to go with him. The other executives were all bringing their wives. He wanted Rebecca to feel proud of him. Maybe spending time together in a beautiful city would help them reconnect. But lately, their arguments had gotten out of hand. He couldn't risk Rebecca making a scene. The pressure of making a major presentation to the whole organization already had him on pins and needles. He wished things were different.

Rebecca had traveled with Robert to his annual work convention several times, and she was especially excited about the trip to Paris. Although she was still angry that he had taken out a loan for his mother without consulting her—they hadn't resolved that situation—she wanted to go with him to Paris. Naturally, she was hurt when he told her she couldn't come.

I used the Catch Method to help Robert and Rebecca resolve their conflict over the convention in Paris. I walked them through the eight steps (covered in detail below), helping them shift into their front brain.

I had them ask open-ended questions to demonstrate their interest in understanding each other's perspectives: "Is there anything else you want me to know?"

This gave them a chance to communicate openly. Robert's unilateral decision to take out a loan was the underlying cause of the offense.

Robert admitted his role in the conflict and asked Rebecca to forgive him. His humility and willingness to make amends initiated the healing process. He also reassured Rebecca that their finances were secure and that he had a plan to pay the loan off in 60 days. Rebecca told Robert that when he took out the loan without confiding in her, she felt unloved, unwanted, unseen, and unheard. It felt like a betrayal. She was so angry that, in the aftermath, nearly any situation left her screaming at him.

It meant so much to Rebecca when Robert admitted that he hadn't been forthright. She was deeply moved when he asked her for forgiveness.

Robert explained to Rebecca how concerned he was about his mother's failing health. He'd taken out the loan to help her pay for a medical procedure with a specialist. This helped Rebecca understand the situation from Robert's point of view.

Using the Catch Method, Robert and Rebecca created an environment that promoted understanding, empathy, and healing, allowed for personal growth, strengthened the bond between them, and set a positive foundation for their future interactions.

The *Catch* Method

1. VALIDATE

2. EMOTIONAL RESPONSE

("TO FEEL ___ IS TO ___")

3. SOFT TOUCH

4. CURIOUS QUESTION

(GOAL IS TO UNDERSTAND, NOT BE UNDERSTOOD)

5. GIVE MORE ROOM TO SHARE

6. REPAIR

(OWN YOUR PART - APOLOGIZE)

7. REASSURE

(WHAT WILL YOU DO DIFFERENT)

8. REACH THROUGH THE PRICKLY

Let's take a look at the eight steps of the Catch Method in detail.

1. **Validate:** Use phrases like "It makes sense that _____" or "I can understand that _____" to validate your partner's perceived truth. Find ways to understand where they're coming from and how they reached their conclusions.

2. **Empathize:** Identify with your partner's emotions so they know that they're not alone in what they're experiencing. This sentence frame may help: "To feel _____in this moment must be _____."

3. **Use soft touch:** It's hard to overestimate the effect of a soft physical touch on someone who's distressed. When children are crying or upset, we intuitively use soft touch to calm them down—pulling them into a hug or caressing their cheek or back. A gentle touch on your partner's hand, arm, or shoulder de-escalates their back brain response and helps ground them in their front brain.

4. **Ask curious questions:** If you don't fully understand your partner's perceptual truth or the story they're telling themselves, ask curious questions. Curious questions have the motivation of seeking to understand rather than to be understood.

5. **Give more room to share:** People sometimes have a lot to say but don't have the space to say it in. Give your partner time and space to speak. Let them know that your priority is to hear what they have to say. Were you able to tell me everything you wanted me to know? Is there anything more?

6. **Repair:** Own your part in the conflict and apologize.

7. **Reassure:** Reassure your partner regarding areas of hurt in the conflict. What will you do differently in the future?

8. **Reach through the prickly:** When one or both of you are in the middle of a protest, your emotions are, as I like to

say, "prickly." Maybe your partner is speaking from their secondary emotion or engaging in their escalated protest behavior. Reaching through the prickly means offering support, validation, and empathy. Create a safe and non-threatening space for dialogue by listening without judgment. Respond with patience and kindness. You probably have an idea of what their primary emotion is even though they aren't expressing it. For example, they may be expressing anger, but you know that usually means they are feeling disrespected. Or they may be showing indifference/coldness which usually shows up when they are hurt. Try addressing the primary emotion instead of responding to anger or coldness, remembering you can help them regulate if you stay regulated. When you and your partner reach through the prickly, tension subsides, and you can express your emotions and needs more openly, vulnerably, and softly.

Since learning the Catch Method, Robert and Rebecca's communication is much better.

Robert feels loved and supported; having support at home has relieved him of much of his stress at work. He's learned to share his feelings in a healthy way rather than simply retreating. Rebecca has learned to better control her emotions and be less confrontational. When Rebecca sees Robert begin to flee, she changes her approach. Instead of assuming that he's rejecting her, she tries to figure out why he's pulling away and considers what he might be going through.

Robert and Rebecca came to me feeling hopeless about their marriage, with just a glimmer of desire to try to make it work. Now, they connect on a daily basis. They feel safe, equipped to face future challenges, and able to encourage each other to do the things they've dreamed of.

When couples approach conflicts with curiosity—just as a detective approaches a crime scene—they start to understand what's happening under the surface of their fights. When they understand the underlying reasons for their behavior and practice the Catch Method, they can develop an altogether new way of handling protests—one that ends in reconnection and burgeoning intimacy. Using the Catch Method will begin a culture of care in your marriage. We begin learning what is underneath the behaviors to a more intimate understanding of insecurities and/or vulnerabilities. The culture of care is helping to care well for your partner when these are activated. Learning to love well is showing that it matters to you, they matter to you, in these moments.

CHAPTER REFLECTION

 You can download a printable version of the Catch Method graphic from www.nakedandexposedbook. com/resources. Practice using the Catch Method to improve your interaction with your partner and build your own connect cycle. You may want to use the cycle you mapped from the previous chapter. Having the sheet in front of you will help. It may feel unnatural and different at first. Wrestling the tendency to not go into the back brain, getting activated, and going back into the old, easy patterns will be challenging. It gets easier over time as the new pathways are forming.

CHAPTER 6:

High Calling: Becoming Healing Partners

. . . .

The Lord God said, "It is not good for the man to be alone.
I will make a helper suitable for him."
GENESIS 2:18

Two are better than one, because they have a good return for
their labor: If either of them falls down, one can help the other
up. But pity anyone who falls and has no one to help them up.
ECCLESIASTES 4:9-10

Cassie and Joe sought counseling from the moment they started their marriage, because in their consideration, divorce was not an option, and they wanted to make sure they were doing marriage right. Although they felt like they had started their marriage with a good connection, they wanted to keep growing and getting better.

89

Unfortunately, as much as they had been proactive in getting counseling, they had still encountered challenges in their marriage. By the time they came to see me, the marriage was almost over. They were each stuck in their own feelings and pain. They wanted to communicate with each other, but they were both too focused on themselves. This disconnect frustrated them. Later, Joe told me that he thought they might not be right for each other and wondered if he should ask for a divorce.

I explained to Cassie and Joe that they could learn how to become healing partners. A healing partner actively supports and contributes to their spouse's emotional well-being, growth, and healing. A healing partner also recognizes and respects their spouse's boundaries, triggers, and individual needs.

We've seen how . . .

- Our brain's emotional development affects our romantic relationships.
- The attachment patterns you created with your parents or primary caregivers transfer to your marriage.
- In a marriage, you need healthy ways to protest—ways that don't disrupt the feeling of safety and security.

We can change ingrained patterns of behavior that run on rigid neural pathways. Old neural pathways never disappear, but the brain is neuroplastic—it has the ability to adapt. The neuroplastic brain creates new neural pathways and strengthens or weakens existing pathways based on experience and learning. In our relationships, these changes take place when we deliberately react and respond in new, healthier ways.

Consider an imaginary couple, Peter and Wendy, who are constantly fighting about dirty dishes. Wendy has asked Peter over and over again to put his dirty dishes in the dishwasher. But somehow, the dishes still end up in the sink or on the counter.

The dirty dishes have become an emotional trigger for stories in Wendy's head: *I'm not being heard. He doesn't care.* Wendy's internal narrative becomes a *pattern* of thought, a rigid neural pathway. Although this hardwired neural pathway will never completely disappear, her primary pattern of thought can be changed by her neuroplastic brain forming a new, different pathway. Neurons that fire together, wire together.

Neuroplasticity is the brain's ability to *change* and *adapt* to the same experiences in a different kind of way

For example, suppose Peter leaves his dishes in the sink— again. This triggers Wendy's negative internal narrative: *He doesn't care about me.* But Wendy realizes that she can create a new pattern of thought by making a deliberate choice to think differently. Although her instinctual back brain kicks into action—something that usually prompts an argument with Peter—she overrides that response and remains in her front brain, intentionally deciding to create an environment of safety and security. She discusses the dishes with Peter with understanding and empathy and learns something about his background that explains why he keeps leaving the dishes in the sink. This new explanation contradicts the old story in her head: *He doesn't care about me.* In addition, because Wendy's response to the dishes in the sink isn't threatening, Peter listens to her protest and reassures her that he *does* care about her.

Wendy's decision to create an atmosphere of safety and security calms Peter's reactionary back brain, avoids a fight, and begins to heal their rigid, negative fight cycle.

The dishwasher story helped Cassie and Joe realize that they could choose new ways of reacting to each other that would promote safety and security when they talked through disagreements—they could become healing partners. They just needed the desire and willingness to change how they reacted to triggering events, creating new, positive neural pathways.

When a threat—for example, the dishes left in the sink—recurs repeatedly over a long period of time—the response to the threat becomes a significant, rigid neural pathway. When the threat presents itself, visceral indicators in the stomach, chest, or throat flare up and the back brain activates. But if we purposefully choose a different approach, we can form new neural pathways.

For example, suppose your spouse tends to flee when you're in the middle of a fight. This triggers your fear of abandonment. But rather than reacting in your back brain, you decide to initiate a new action tendency—you reach out to your spouse for reassurance and soothing. This creates a new neural pathway that, over time, can become the new primary and automatic pathway, overriding the old one.

When you and your spouse co-regulate each other's emotions in moments of conflict, you're doing more than just calming your back-brain reactions; you're also helping each other rewire your brains.

Three Ways to Rewire Your Brain

There are three primary ways to rewire the neural pathways in your brain: self, God, and spouse.

1. Self

The first way to rewire your brain is through your own individual effort. You can use self-help or counseling to gain an understanding of when, how, and why your back-brain response is triggered.

When an event triggers the fight, flee, or freeze response in your amygdala, you have a rewiring opportunity. Instead of allowing the ingrained pathway to fire and reinforce itself, you can practice self-regulation skills you've learned from professional counselors who utilize empirically supported interventions.

You can learn to recognize the bodily sensations that accompany events that trigger your back brain—a gut punch, tightening in the chest, rapid heartbeat, or a lump in the throat. These physical signals then alert you that you need to intentionally regulate your back-brain response and reconnect with your front brain.

Through consistent practice—repeatedly engaging your front brain and intentionally choosing responses that promote connection and growth—you form new neural pathways, ones that enable healthier, more adaptive patterns of behavior.

Many people begin the work of improving their marriage by embarking on a personal journey of self-improvement, using techniques like:

- Mindfulness
- Meditation
- Journaling
- Cognitive behavioral therapy (CBT)
- Eye movement desensitization and reprocessing (EMDR)
- Talk therapy
- Counseling

These tools and outside help aid in self-regulation in the face of threats or challenges. A skilled counselor can be a partner for practicing emotional co-regulation, provide a safe and supportive space for processing emotions, and introduce front-brain interventions that promote co-regulation and facilitate healing.

We can learn to become our own *self-soothers* in times of *distress*

The aforementioned interventions—backed by scientific research and rooted in biblical principles—have the power to reshape your brain and transform your relationships. You can learn to self-soothe when you're distressed. A journey of self-discovery cultivates resilience and positively impacts your relationships and overall well-being.

2. God

The second way to rewire your brain is through your relationship with God.

Researchers have explored how people connect with God as an attachment figure.[1] People of faith view God much as they view a primary caregiver: As their heavenly Father, He provides care and comfort in times of need. Just like a primary caregiver or a romantic partner, God provides us with a safe haven and a secure base in times of emotional and physical distress.

Suppose something happens that causes you to feel unsafe or insecure. Your back brain is activated, and your instinct is to fight, flee, or freeze (whatever your tendency is).

Our faith informs us that God can ground us in peace, calm, assurance, and joy. Our God is an entity greater than ourselves, and we can reach out to Him. Just like a physical father, our heavenly Father responds with comfort and care. He tells us that we matter to Him; He will never leave or forsake us.

Instead of remaining in your back-brain reaction to your situation, you can exercise your faith to reach out to God through spiritual disciplines. Some suggestions to name a few are:

- Prayer
- Worship
- Bible reading

Reaching out to God in your distress is a second channel through which you can rewire your brain. When you're unsure of a relationship or feeling threatened, God can assuage your feelings and reassure you.

> Through our faith practices, our connection with God is curative for our emotional and attachment wounds

3. Spouse

The third way to create neurological thought patterns is for you and your spouse to become healing partners. [2]

When you and your spouse are healing partners, you respond to each other's protests in a healthy way. Instead of allowing free rein to your back-brain reaction to a disagreement, you respond in your front brain and provide love, empathy, comfort, and care. This creates a sense of safety and security, allows you to co-regulate your emotions, and rewires your brain with new, positive neural pathways.

Suppose a couple has a history of being locked in a rigid, negative fight cycle. As they learn to be healing partners, their brains become less reactionary, because they're rewiring the old, back-brain fight cycle with the foundations of a safe and secure relationship.

Attachment science shows us that we're hardwired for belonging and connection; that's why our brain's emotional development is inextricably linked to co-regulating our emotions with our primary caregivers. Although a couple may have spent years mired in a rigid, reactionary, back-brain fight cycle, as healing partners they can learn to reprocess their triggers and respond to each other in less reactionary ways. This creates safety and security in the relationship, which, in turn, softens strident protests or lessens the urge to shut down in moments of conflict.

Research has shown that the most effective way to rewire the brain in order to rebuild a romantic relationship is for spouses to become healing partners. All three healing pathways are helpful, but you and your spouse working together has the greatest impact on your relationship. Said another way, of all three healing pathways, research reveals that your partner is the most effective one to provide you the ability to rewire your neural pathways and create new ones.[3]

As your healing partner, your spouse can . . .

- Help you understand your thoughts, emotions, and experiences.
- Help you see things from a different angle.
- Help you analyze your assumptions.
- Offer validation and empathy.
- Allow space to share and be heard.

Our partner has the greatest capacity to trigger the amygdala more than any other person due to this attachment having the most meaning to us. This means we have the greatest capacity to feel or experience our most vulnerable and/or sensitive emotional insecurities in the context of this relationship. When this occurs, our spouse can also be the tangible, concrete comforter in the presence of this triggering. The process of sharing vulnerabilities while met with empathy from your partner brings healing.4 So even if these are vulnerabilities developed from within the relationship or those we experienced from other relationships, our spouse can still be the agent of healing for each of these. Our reactionary brain becomes less reactive over time in these areas. It is a process of frequency, duration, and intensity. Said another way, over time you won't get triggered as often, it won't last as long or feel as emotionally intense.

> **Our *spouse* has the capacity to have the *greatest impact* toward our *healing* than any other**

When spouses interact as healing partners, they develop a more balanced and nuanced perception of themselves and their interactions. Ultimately, they create a deeper, more intimate bond.

Forging a Healing Partnership

The research confirms what we already know from the Bible. In the first chapter of the first book of the Bible, God creates man in His image for his pleasure (Genesis 1:26) and says that His creation is "very good" (v. 31). It is a similar scenario of your desire to have your own children which has similar images to both parents and the feelings you draw when looking and watching them. Do you recognize the similarities of attachment to the parent/child research as well as the relationship between God and man/woman?

Soon after, God declares that this isn't enough. Man needs more: "It is not good for the man to be alone. I will make a helper suitable for him" (Genesis 2:18). Ecclesiastes 4:9-10 adds, "Two are better than one. If either of them falls down, one can help the other up."

God formed woman out of man for companionship, a differentiating kind of love, pleasure and functional partnership including procreation. The first "marriage" was two people from one flesh (Genesis 2:21-23). From that point on, marriage is a reflection of this same flesh attachment of two people coming together to be one flesh. God gave this uniquely special relationship one thing that differentiates it from any other relationship – sexual expression and union. This is a pleasurable outward expression of one's flesh, a beautiful symbol of this deeply inner representation of the love and attachment of one flesh. God sent the Holy Spirit, Himself, to reside in us (1 Corinthians 6:19) and tasked us to love our spouse as Jesus loves the church, his bride (Ephesians 5:25). We, as our God-designed and given gift for our spouse, are His representatives to be the tangible presence to love in concrete ways that even God cannot – in the flesh. Research and the Bible point to the same thing. Spouses are instruments of healing to one another and the most effective of the three. This is a high calling.

God/Man/Us Lily Pad

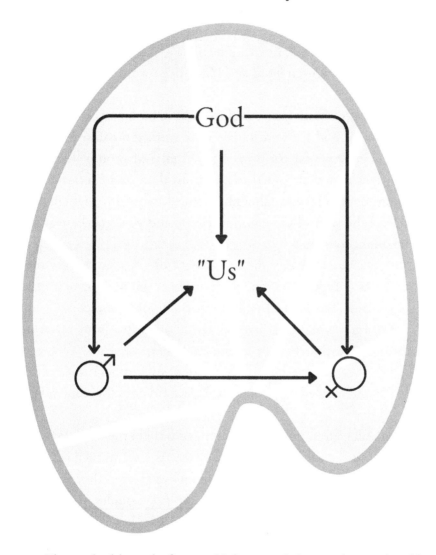

This is the lily pad of marital life as God designed – God, Self and Partner. This is the design of symbolic book ends of adult married life. The beginning and the end. As you will see in the next section, all other things come and go or change, but these are the sustenance throughout. Please note the similarities on the lily pad. They correspond to what shows up in the research of neuroscience of healing pathways – God, Self and Partner. The two, God's word and His creation (Bible and science), do not contradict. God's written word and His spoken word are one and the same.

Forming a healing partnership requires both partners to cooperate. Cassie and Joe were all in, so we worked on all three fronts to form new neural pathways: self, God, and spouse. It is very important that these practices aren't just done as a check the box but are done long enough and practiced frequently enough that you feel the shift of the emotional state and you feel the reactive back brain soothed.

- For example, on the individual front, Cassie realized that as a Type A person, she wanted to be in control all the time. She learned to lean into his comfort and care.
- They began to experience one another in a more reverent, spiritual way – as a calling and a purpose.
- They became intimately aware of each other's insecurities and learned to move towards each other in those moments.

Initially, given the dark places they'd been in their relationship, Cassie and Joe thought they were crazy. As they worked on their relationship, they realized that they aren't as crazy as they thought. Everyone brings baggage into a relationship. Couples just need to have the willingness to work on those things. There is always hope for your marriage.

The Us Flowchart goes on to illustrate the order of creation and their priority. God instructed this first union to multiply with children (Genesis 1:28). He, then, instructed them to take dominion over his creation (Genesis 1:28). This can mean:

- Enjoy Recreation and Leisure (Genesis 1:21). I take pleasure in watching you enjoy what I created for you, my master playground.
- Work (Genesis 3:17; Psalms 90:17). Go use your gifts and abilities I gave you for provision and giving back.
- Church and Service (Hebrews 10:25; Galatians 5:13-14). Don't neglect meeting together for encouragement and service.
- Family and Extended Family (Psalms 68:6; Proverbs 27:9). I made you for connection and community so find your tribe.

The bottom portion of the Us Flowchart, below the lily pad, reflects portions of our life that move and change, come and go. They cannot take precedence or priority over the lily pad. They are the enhancers of life, not sustenance.

Us Flowchart

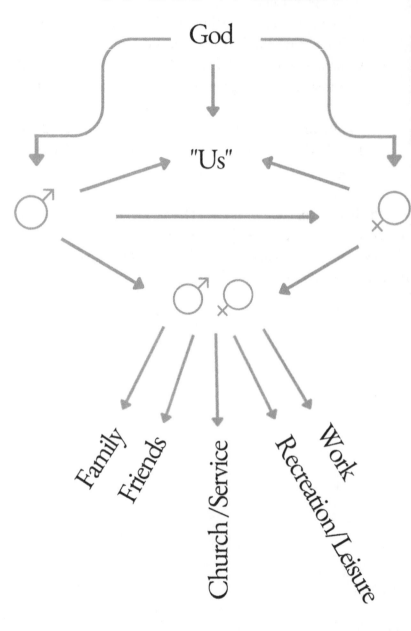

Of course, it's ideal for couples to use every means available to rewire their brains if they're stuck in a negative fight cycle. If you and your spouse practice self-regulating, spiritual disciplines like prayer and worship, *and* learn to be healing partners, neither of you will have to bear the full weight of responsibility for your relationship. This can be the differentiation between interdependence and codependence. That's a good thing—because no one can suddenly override their back-brain reaction every time there's conflict. But forming a healing partnership is indispensable.

Let's review some of the things that happen when spouses become healing partners:

- When couples work together to co-regulate their emotions, they create safety and security and reduce stress.
- This alleviates the back brain's stress response and grounds each partner in their front brain.
- When couples connect in the front brain, the area of higher reasoning, they're soft- spoken, trusting, vulnerable, and able to solve problems.
- Consequently, conflicts don't end in reactive, back-brain disconnection. They end in front-brain reconnection.
- When the marriage is healthy, spouses do better regulating themselves. They're more focused at work and at home, sleep better at night, and have a positive impact on their general health and well-being. The effects spill over to other relationships, too.

Cassie discovered what was triggering her and why she was reacting poorly. She explained what she learned to Joe, which helped him empathize with her and break out of his own feelings and perceptions. He saw how his actions affected Cassie. Now, Joe feels like he can hear and serve Cassie better.

Cassie and Joe's story illustrates some of the ways couples can become healing partners.

CHAPTER REFLECTION

 Whether you caused your partner's wounds or not, you can become their healing partner by providing safety, security, and emotional co-regulation. With this new mindset, you can realize the full power the relationship with your spouse can become. Again, this is a high calling.

CHAPTER 7:

Healing Conversations:
Repairing Your Marriage

. . . .

Do not let any unwholesome talk come out of your mouths, but
only what is helpful for building others up according to their
needs, that it may benefit those who listen.

EPHESIANS 4:29

Brene Brown's research[1] in the arena of vulnerability and shame provides resounding evidence that shame, guilt, and hurt are healed through vulnerability, acceptance, and compassion.

When the biblical Adam and Eve didn't do what was asked of them, their response was to cover their nakedness and hide from God. They also developed defense mechanisms to cover their shame—Adam blamed Eve, and Eve blamed the serpent. Blaming others is a natural human tendency.

Paul and Sara were working on overcoming betrayal wounds from a couple of years earlier in their marriage. Through counseling, they had made it past the initial crisis. But periodically, something would trigger the old wounds and cause challenges to their relationship. They came to me looking for tools to improve their marriage.

If a couple doesn't process a betrayal in a way that restores their closeness and fosters a pathway for forgiveness, they retain the memory of the incident for their self-protection. There is a definitive path to do this well that will be necessary with a skilled, seasoned licensed professional therapist that is trained in this area. Without someone to help on this path of healing, more harm can actually happen in the aftermath.

> **Vulnerability is the *key* that builds *intimacy***

That's what happened with Paul and Sara. This is just a small snapshot within their journey:

- Sara felt betrayed and lived in shame.
- Paul felt guilty and continually apologized to Sara for everything.

It's difficult to learn how to have safe conversations; it's even more difficult to learn to have safe conversations that bring you back to a moment of betrayal.

Healing Conversations

So far we have worked on:

- Identifying the disconnect cycle of communication.
- Building a connect cycle of communication.
- Shaping a new mindset of healing partnership within the relationship.

It is time, now, to work backwards in the relationship. We have formed a more safe and secure way of interacting with one another and forged a culture of care within the relationship. Once this is done, we have to revisit old pain points of the relationship and have a more corrective, healing conversation around that time or event using the new method of interaction. This will get a different result, allow movement forward for healing and forgiveness, open up avenues of work through solutions, deepen the intimacy, and begin restoring levels of trust. Many couples seem reluctant to open up old wounds especially if they are experiencing the embryonic newness of connection in their marriages. They are hesitant to open a can of worms during calm moments in their relationship. However, as painful as this may seem, it has to be done. Old pain wounds in the relationship resurface and when they do, they come at surprising times and with intensity.

Having the deliberate and controlled conversation with intention allows one to prepare mentally and have the ability to show up for their partner with more safe and secure resolve. These conversations are able to help reduce the potential reactivity of the back brain in other moments. It also allows the forgiveness process to begin. Notice, I said process.

Forgiveness is a process; it's not a one-time, one-and-done event. They're a bit like immunizations—giving someone a tiny dose of a viral or bacterial agent so they begin to build immunity to it. A healing conversation is similar; it pricks an old wound. After a healing conversation around a past pain point, the wounded person is in a different emotional state when something triggers those memories. Healing conversations use the same method of the connect cycle as demonstrated and learned in Chapter 5.

Paul's betrayal had rocked Sara and Paul's marriage. They knew they had to find a way to heal and rebuild their relationship. The affair had taken place at a difficult time in their marriage. Paul loved Sara and never intended to hurt her. When she found out about it, he immediately ended the relationship and went into counseling with Sara. His guilt was consuming him. Paul hoped their intensive with me would help them reconnect and rebuild the intimate bond they once had.

A Healing Conversation: Paul and Sara

I taught Paul and Sara the Catch Method. Using those principles, they embarked on a journey of healing. Here's one of their healing conversations.

Paul: "I understand how much pain my actions caused you. I realize that my betrayal shattered the trust we had in our marriage."

Sara: "It's difficult to put into words how much it hurt when I found out. I felt completely broken and lost."

Paul: *Soft touch on Sara's hand.* "I'm committed to rebuilding what we had. I know words alone won't undo the pain, but I hope this touch reminds you that I'm here to support you and comfort you in any way I can."

Sara: *Tearfully.* "It means a lot to me that you're willing to try. It's been hard for me to trust you again."

Paul: "I know we have a long way to go."

Sara: "I feel like the foundation of our marriage was shattered. I don't see you in the same way anymore. I will need reassurance now and from time to time that you're truly committed to rebuilding trust and that it won't happen again."

Paul: "I take full responsibility for my actions, and I'm committed to making things right. I want to work on rebuilding your trust, not just through words, but through actions that show my love and commitment to you."

Sara: "It's going to take time; I want to believe that we can heal from this. I need you to keep showing up and working on our relationship, even when it gets tough."

Paul: "I promise to do everything in my power to make our love and connection stronger than ever before. You are my priority, and I will do whatever it takes to repair the damage I've caused."

Sara: "Hearing your commitment gives me hope."

Paul: "I believe in us; I want to rebuild our marriage and create a better future together. I'm grateful for your forgiveness and the opportunity to start over again."

Paul and Sara created a safe space to address the issue that was tearing their marriage apart. They each listened to the other's perspective. They gave each other space to communicate openly. They found solace in reassuring each other of their enduring love, desire, and commitment to meeting each other's needs. Using the Catch Method and intentional healing conversations, they created an environment of understanding, empathy, and healing.

> Intentional *healing* conversations around past pain points in the relationship can start the *forgiveness process*

Through the intensive, Paul and Sara were equipped to heal their marriage:

- Before the intensive, Sara saw Paul as a villain. Their sensitivities from the betrayal prevented them from having any difficult conversations. Consequently, many situations went unresolved. In the intensive, they learned to slow down, use the Catch Method, and think about what their words and body language were communicating to the other person.

- The basics of neuroscience helped them understand that when our back brain is triggered, we stop thinking rationally. Paul and Sara realized they could be healing partners; no one else could help them co-regulate in the same way. As a result, they recognized the need to turn *toward* instead of *away* from each other in times of conflict.

- Using the Catch Method, Paul learned how to validate Sara's concerns and to speak love to her in ways that work for her. He learned to lean into disagreements and work on the issue at hand. They learned to leave past issues out of their present conversations— that way, they could focus on the conflict at hand, each seeking to understand the other's perspective.

- Sara learned to reach toward Paul softly for reassurance when triggered while Paul owned the opportunity to provide her a source of comfort rather than a reinforcement of the pain.

- Paul and Sara prioritize making time to connect. They pursue each other—in a good way—when they haven't had a chance to connect for a few days.

Today, Paul and Sara feel like their marriage is thriving, and they feel like they're closer than they've ever been.

Pain or betrayal points—whether from past or current relationships—affect many couples. As was the case for Sara and Paul, many things trigger these old wounds, and couples relive them over and over again. If you and your partner have any such wounds, it's crucial to have deliberate, healing conversations around them so they don't keep affecting your relationship.

A Healing Conversation: Jody and Tim

Healing conversations take various forms depending on each couple's unique dynamics and needs.

Shortly after Jody and Tim got together, Jody took up golf. Why? Because golf was important to Tim. However, she wasn't nearly as good at it; she took three swings to every one of his. She was always running ahead, looking for where her errant strokes had landed.

One day, Tim didn't wait for her to get out of the way before taking a swing; he thought the ball would sail over her. Instead, the ball hit Jody on the head. Jody fell over, holding her head in pain.

Tim came running over. "Are you okay?" he asked, feeling awful.

"I'm here learning how to play golf—just for you—and you can't even wait for me to get out of the way?!" Jody yelled.

Tim was horrified. "I'm so sorry," he said. "I didn't mean to hit you. I thought the ball would go over your head. I won't ever do that again."

Twenty years later, any time Jody thought Tim was being impatient, she would ask him, "Remember the golf ball?"

That was their code for, "Tim, be patient with me."

"Absolutely, honey," Tim would say. "I remember the golf ball. Can you believe I took that swing before you were out of the way?"

And with that, they'd be back on track. How did a reference to a past traumatic event become a humorous and effective use of the Catch Method?

Tim and Jody got to that point by having a healing conversation. They created a new story. If Tim's impatience prompts Jody to protest, they don't need a long discussion. They don't even need to talk about what's happening in the present. They use the Catch Method and have a brief, safe and secure conversation about a long-ago misaimed golf ball. Their golf ball conversation quickly restores their relationship; it's a personal language between them that allows them to overcome current triggers.

After you've had meaningful healing conversations over past wounds or betrayals in your marriage, things will still occasionally prick those wounds. But over time, the triggers will come less frequently. When they do come, you can move past them more quickly. The emotional intensity associated with the betrayal or wound diminishes.

That's forgiveness; it's a process. The process involves handling triggers with intentionality, not letting them boil over into back-brain replays of past pain.

"Remember the golf ball?" means, "Hey, you're being impatient."

The response isn't, "That was 20 years ago! Haven't you forgiven me yet?" The response is, "I remember"—which really means, "I hear your protest, and I'll slow down."

There's a protest, a catch, and immediate reconnection and comfort.

Many couples come to counseling wanting to learn how to communicate better. First, I help them understand their fight cycle. Then we look at their areas of vulnerability. We study how they show up when they're triggered. They each learn the language of their partner's protests; then they can practice responding to protests in ways that build a more safe and secure connect cycle and develop a culture of care.

A culture of care involves more than *doing* things for each other; it's about understanding each other and appreciating who you *are* to each other.

As a counselor (and out of curiosity), I study behavior. I watch other couples when I'm out in social settings and the community. I'm also a sucker for "reality" shows centered around love and romance. Based on the ratings I see, I don't think I'm alone in that. Most people want a romantic connection. We notice when a couple has it, and we notice when they don't. In your marriage, don't settle for anything less than what God created, designed, and hardwired you to have.

> Couples deepen their *culture of care* through a shared understanding of just *what* they do, but *who* they are for one another

Learning to love well is hard work and takes time, but it will have a lasting impact on your life. I've never yet met a couple that put in the work and said it wasn't worth it. Developing this culture of care takes time but deepens the intimate bond of knowing each other.

CHAPTER REFLECTION

Safe and secure healing conversations around past pain points in a relationship diminish the frequency and emotional intensity of events that trigger the old wounds.

CHAPTER 8:

The Intimacy for Life Method™ — Protecting Attachment Using Renewal Systems

· · · · · · · · · · · ·

Above all, love each other deeply, because love
covers over a multitude of sins.
1 PETER 4:8

May your fountain be blessed, and may you rejoice
in the wife of your youth.
PROVERBS 5:18

Couples coming in for counseling often mention ongoing issues in various areas: finances, sex, dealing with in-laws, parenting roles, and the need for personal time. However, there's usually quite a bit going on under the surface of these issues.

The Bucket System

In my counseling, I follow a three-step process that I call "The Bucket System." Each step covers a "bucket" full of various aspects of a couple's relationship. The three buckets provide a structure for exploring and addressing different areas of concern.

Let's take a closer look at the three buckets.

Bucket One

Bucket One holds the stressors and conflict points that couples commonly argue about. This bucket is for areas that tend to cause tension and disagreements. For most couples, it includes topics like finances, sex, dealing with in-laws, parenting roles, personal time, role division and hobbies.

Bucket Two

Bucket Two holds the ways couples *navigate* and *communicate* about the stressors and conflict points in Bucket One. When we work on Bucket Two, we get into communication patterns, relationship dynamics, and the recurring fight cycles that emerge during conflicts. If you want to establish safe and secure ways of resolving issues as a couple, you have to have understanding in addressing these patterns.

Bucket Three

Bucket Three holds the systems of renewal within a relationship. When we work on Bucket Three, I help couples cultivate practices and activities that counteract their stressors and fight cycles. These renewal systems foster intimacy, connection, and strength. Renewal systems include emotional engagement, shared recreational activities, spiritual intimacy, finding shared meaning and purpose, and physical and sexual intimacy.

Working with the Buckets

I usually begin my counseling by working on Bucket Two, focusing on creating a safe and secure way of talking about and resolving conflicts. Once we've ironed out the dynamics of their communication, a couple can effectively discuss the stressors in Bucket One. We take each of the stressors one by one from Bucket One and feed it through their new cycle of communication formed in Bucket Two. The work on Buckets One and Two produces a stronger sense of safety and security in the relationship, and that leads naturally to a desire for deeper emotional engagement, shared leisure activities, exploration of spiritual intimacy, and enhanced physical and sexual connection. It has been my experience that some counselors will go directly to Bucket One and begin a process of negotiating contractual terms of agreement on the stressors of disagreement. This is a faulty approach. Understanding and shifting the underlying emotions of these topics is a must first step before any couple can legitimately shift the "want to" to show up differently in the areas of contention and disagreement which happens in the work of Bucket Two, first. Likewise, some counselors want to jump to Bucket Three prescriptively scheduling time for the renewal systems we are about to discuss. It isn't a matter of just scheduling "date night." There is a reason that couples don't already engage in these systems naturally. They are not unintelligent people. They just lost the "want to." Without taking the proper steps to help these emotional states shift, developing a more safe and secure communication cycle, and reigniting the

> We have to *shift* the stories and the emotions *first* before we get to the *business of marriage*

"want to," couples will not "want to" nor engage long term in these activities. This is the reason that these areas show up last in the order of discussion.

Progress on the contents of one bucket depends on progress with the others; it's interdependent. De-escalating the fight cycle in Bucket Two and effectively addressing stressors from Bucket One creates a solid foundation for vulnerability, connection, and renewal—Bucket Three.

Case Study: Cheryl and Chris

Cheryl and Chris met when they were 21 and 22, respectively, and got married about two years later. When I met them, they had been married for seven years, had three kids, and were completely broken.

They were still married, but they weren't living together. During that seventh year of marriage, all the issues they hadn't worked through boiled up to the surface. Instead of working things out, they pushed each other away and separated. They had signed paperwork to start the divorce process, and their kids were brokenhearted.

Cheryl was pushing for a divorce. She felt like their problems were too thorny to fix, and she didn't want to deal with them.

"I'll try one last thing," she told Chris, "but then I'm moving on." That's when they came to me. Cheryl ended up storming out of that first session—but she also realized that she wanted to try to repair their marriage. She just didn't know where to start.

Over the next six months, Chris and Cheryl did everything I recommended, and by the end of that time, they were reconciled and living together again. A year later, they renewed their marriage vows. Their relationship was full of joy and intimacy they'd never known before, because they had worked through all the hidden, underlying issues.

As Chris and Cheryl worked to renew their own relationship, they renewed their relationship with God, too. Their own healing process forced them to rely on God. As their faith grew, they told God they would do anything He asked of them, because they were so thankful that He showed up when they needed Him most. God called them to become foster parents. After a few years, they adopted one of their foster children.

Think about that—they allowed God to work in their lives, to heal their marriage. In response, they opened to God, and He directed them into fostering. Ultimately, healing their marriage paved the way for a little boy—their adopted son—to have a family. God truly made beauty from their ashes.

Working with Cheryl and Chris was a true gift. I witnessed them working on their own relationship, coming together again, and reaching beyond themselves. At that stage, they wanted a more intimate connection. That's when we began to work on Bucket Three: renewal systems.

Renewal Systems

Renewal systems are the behaviors and rituals that counteract the stressors of life, nurture your relationship, and guard it against everything that life throws your way. Renewal systems bring you and your spouse back to your lily pad to develop your life together—just the two of you.

When you enter counseling, most therapists will say, "If you do *x*, *y*, and *z*, things will be good." In other words, they're saying, "Put these things into place, and your marriage will change."

- For instance, you may have heard, "Couples that pray together, stay together." So, there you go: just pray. If you pray together, your marriage will repair itself.
- Or you may have heard, "Never stop dating your spouse." Schedule a weekly date night, and your marriage will improve.

Don't get me wrong—it's good for couples to pray together and go on dates. However, the fact that these things disappear from or don't develop in a marriage isn't the *source* of a couple's problems; it's a *symptom*.

In our hearts, we know much of what needs to happen in a healthy relationship. The problem with many couples is that they just don't *want* to do those things; they've lost their "want to."

The first thing a couple who's doing things out of obligation needs is an emotional shift—back toward *wanting* to show up, toward a *desire* for Bucket Three items like vulnerability, connection, and renewal. When you're stuck in a rigid fight cycle, you lose or never develop the things in Bucket Three. Fight cycles erode intimacy and the desire to do things that keep relationships healthy and vibrant.

When we break the fight cycle, we de-escalate prickly secondary emotions and start to move from the back brain into the front brain. Once we've restored calm and front-brain reasoning skills, you can work through problems, hear perspectives other than your own, and have healing conversations. The rigid, negative stories that have been running in your heads during your fight cycle revert back to your original storyline—the stories that brought you together, helped you fall in love, and made you *willingly* vow to care for each other on your wedding day.

Your "want to" returns.

Now we've reached a point where we can do more than mere remediation. We can begin to develop renewal systems and deep, abiding intimacy.

We're designed to connect deeply with one person of our choosing, for life. In this special relationship, we connect with our partner emotionally, mentally, spiritually, and physically. As you develop renewal systems, you'll intentionally incorporate each of these connection points into your relationship, maintaining a sense of closeness and vitality. Ultimately, renewal systems foster your growth individually and as a couple and fuel the continuing escalation of intimacy.

> There are three levels of communication in marriage... *transactional*, *monitoring protests*, and *emotional engagement*

Renewal systems require ongoing intentional effort. I recommend regularly evaluating the state of your relationship to identify areas that can benefit from increased attention and renewal.

The Intimacy for Life Method™

I created the Intimacy for Life Method™ to help couples reconnect and reestablish their intimate bond. The Intimacy for Life Method™ will enhance your marriage on many levels, teaching you . . .

> The Intimacy for Life Method™ involves *emotional* engagement, *recreational* and *leisure* partnering, shared *spiritual* practices and purpose, and *physical* and *sexual* affection

- How neuroscience shows that we're created for connection
- How and why we get disconnected
- How to restore a lost connection, making it better than ever
- How to break the fight cycle and manage internal and external stressors
- How to create a culture of care and communication that enables problem solving and healing conversations
- How to shift away from negative internal narratives and soothe painful emotions, restoring closeness and the desire to care for each other
- How to develop systems that protect an intimate marriage bond, ensuring longevity and deep satisfaction

Some couples may need the help of a well-trained, knowledgeable, seasoned therapist to guide them through the Intimacy for Life Method™, but others may be able to work through the steps independently.

Emotional Engagement

Emotional engagement is thorough communication with your partner that deepens your relationship. When you're emotionally engaged, you show vulnerability in the things you tell your partner.

Set aside dedicated time to connect on an emotional level. Have in-depth conversations in which you share your thoughts, feelings, and experiences with each other. Actively listen and show empathy, seeking to understand and validate each other's emotions. This emotional connection builds trust and intimacy.

Here are some ideas for initiating and deepening emotional engagement in your marriage:

- Ask your partner about their thoughts, feelings, or experiences on a topic that is important to both of you.

- Share your emotions and invite your partner to do the same. Express how you feel about a particular situation or aspect of your relationship.
- Discuss a cherished memory—a special trip, meaningful event, or moment of shared joy. Share how that memory makes you feel and ask your partner to share their emotions and thoughts about it.
- Discuss the ups and downs of your day with your partner. Talk about the challenges you faced and the victories you achieved.
- Express empathy and support for each other. Offer encouragement and validation.
- Celebrate each other's successes. Provide comfort or assistance when your partner is facing difficulties.

Recreational and Leisure Partnering

When was the last time you went out together and just had fun? Recreation and leisure are important in establishing intimacy.

It's common for women to crave an emotional connection, but many men want a recreational partner. Men may struggle with doing the eyeball-to-eyeball thing; they want a side-by-side thing—and that's okay. There's a time and a place for both.

Men experience ultimate contentment when they're involved in shared recreational activities with their partner. When you and your partner enjoy a fun, de-stressing activity together, you see each other in new ways. You break the monotony of daily life, unload the heavy stuff you're always carrying, and just have fun. If you don't already have a shared activity, try something new together. You can both learn at the same time.

Here are some ideas for recreational and leisure activities you can enjoy together:

- Go for a hike or take a nature walk in a local park.
- Take a scenic bike ride together.
- Go on a camping trip or have a picnic in the great outdoors.
- Try a water activity like kayaking, paddleboarding, or canoeing.
- Exploring new places through road trips or weekend getaways.
- Take a fitness class together—yoga, dance, or martial arts.
- Play tennis, golf, basketball, or soccer as a couple or with other couples.
- Go for regular walks, runs, or bike rides in your neighborhood or nearby parks.
- Take art classes together—learn painting, pottery, or sculpting.
- Do a home improvement project together.
- Cook or bake together. Try out new recipes, or experiment with different cuisines.
- Go to concerts or theater shows together.
- Explore museums, art galleries, or cultural exhibitions.
- Watch a movie or binge-watch a TV series as a cozy night-in activity.
- Go to comedy clubs or participate in open mic nights.
- Find new music, books, or podcasts and discuss them together.

Spiritual Intimacy

In our spiritual practices, we seek meaning and purpose in life. We experience life on a higher, sacred dimension. Spiritual intimacy involves practices that connect us to God, and it encompasses the belief that we're placed on earth for a purpose larger than ourselves.

This involves internal spiritual practices couples engage in together for their own personal renewal connection, as well as practices they engage in externally that bring a sense of purpose and meaning to the "why" they were placed together. Engaging in a shared purpose deepens their connection and desire to the union – a sense of calling. They develop an understanding of why God put them together and are able to do something greater together than what they can do apart.

We develop spiritual intimacy by sharing our inner thoughts and experiences in this realm with our partner.

Here are some activities you and your partner can use to cultivate spiritual intimacy:

- Engage in daily prayer or meditation sessions as a couple.
- Read and discuss sacred texts or religious literature together.
- Participate in spiritual retreats or workshops.
- Set aside specific times for joint devotion or worship.
- Attend religious services together.
- Get involved in volunteer activities or community service projects through your religious institution.
- Join a small group or study circle focused on spiritual growth and exploration.
- Schedule study sessions with other couples who share similar spiritual interests.
- Participate in group activities like prayer circles, guided meditations, or spiritual rituals.
- Share reflections from your personal studies, devotions, or meditation.
- Listen to an inspirational message together.
- Use music to worship together.
- Bond with each other through your shared awe of God's beautiful creation.

- Serve together in an organization in which you share an interest.

Physical and Sexual Affection

Physical affection is the physical expression of care and comfort within the marital relationship, and it involves much more than sex. Physical and sexual affection is a set of behaviors on a continuum of rhythms developed on one end from non-sexual affection such as habitual kisses and hugs of good-byes and hellos, contact

> God's *design* for *sexual* fulfillment was for mutual *pleasure*

throughout the day, all the way through the sexual expression such as sexual bids, fore-play, and sometimes penetrative intercourse which at times may lead to mutual orgasm.

God is the master designer of both the attachment co-regulation system, which involves physical touch, *and* the sexual relationship in marriage, a relationship intended both for reproduction and, more frequently, for pleasure. The God-designed sexual relationship in marriage differentiates marriage from every other human relationship. Sexual intimacy is multi- layered and complex. Due to the delicate nature of this act mentally, emotionally, spiritually, and physically there are many couples that can suffer from their own unique challenges. This is not meant as an over-simplification of this. There are real challenges that have real pain for some couples. There is a unique sexual cycle of communication for couples in this area that may need time, attention, and delicacy to help map and understand. Some couples may need the help of a well-versed therapist to help in the pain and shame of these mental, emotional, and physical challenges.

Here are suggested ways to incorporate physical and sexual affection into your marriage:

- Embrace each other in warm and affectionate hugs, holding each other closely.
- Cuddle on the couch or in bed, enjoying physical closeness and intimacy.
- Touch or gently caress each other to express care and love.
- Exchange passionate kisses that communicate desire, love, and connection.
- Hold hands while walking or sitting together.
- Snuggle up together while watching a movie or reading a book.
- Engage in activities that involve touch—dancing, exercising, or doing yoga together.
- Engage in sexual activity that is mutually consensual, pleasurable, and satisfying.
- Express your attraction and desire for each other through flirtatious gestures, compliments, and playful banter.
- Send each other affectionate texts or love notes to express your longing for physical connection.
- Plan romantic dates or weekend getaways that create an atmosphere of intimacy and physical connection.

Fostering intimacy and maintaining a strong connection in a lifelong relationship requires ongoing dedication, effort, and mutual support.

By incorporating the practices this book has covered into your marriage—practices like maintaining open communication, resolving conflicts, spending quality time together, fostering emotional connection, and staying physically and sexually affectionate—you and your partner can nurture the bond between you and experience intimacy for life.

The journey of intimacy is unique for each couple. Intimacy requires active participation, adaptability, and a deep commitment to understanding and meeting each other's needs. But with love, patience, and a mutual desire for growth, you and your partner can create a lasting and fulfilling marriage—a relationship that builds intimacy for life.

CHAPTER REVIEW

 Incorporating the four components of the Intimacy for Life Method™ into your marriage will help you maintain a healthier, more satisfying relationship. For a deeper dive, be on the lookout for my next book that further details The Intimacy for Life Method.™

How well are you and your partner doing on your journey toward intimacy for life? Find out by taking a free assessment at:

www.nakedandexposed.com/assessment.

NOW THAT YOU HAVE READ THE BOOK, HERE IS WHAT'S NEXT:

1. **Take the Marriage Assessment.** Based on the research presented in this book, I devised a marriage assessment that gauges the current state of your marriage. You can access the Marriage Assessment and other free resources at: www.nakedandexposedbook.com/resources.

2. **Subscribe to my podcast.** Join me weekly as I host open discussions around creating the kind of marriage God designed through teaching, interviews, and testimonials of real couples I've worked with on *The Love Leading Podcast with Dr. Shanon*. You can subscribe and listen on all podcast platforms.

3. **Sign up for my webinar** at: https://www.shanonrobertscounseling.com/webinar.

4. Share the book with a friend.

ACKNOWLEDGMENTS

First and foremost, I want to acknowledge all my couples. Thank you for trusting me into such sensitive, personal space and the courage it takes to walk this path. It is always such a humble honor to be on the front row watching miracles and healing happen. I never take it for granted. I have learned as much from you as I pray you have learned with me. You each hold a tenderly fond place in my heart.

I would be amiss to not mention my ultimate loves, my three children, Bailey, Jake and Cade. Thank you for teaching me how to love deeply. Thank you for the opportunity of seeing first-hand how this attachment science works in the real world! Life on this planet would not be as bright without you in it. I love being your mother.

Thanks to the best writing coach and publisher, Cheli Grace. Without you, this book would have never materialized. You have such a balance of warmth and professionalism. Your patient and caring support is so appreciated. If I had a dime for every time you calmed me down or said, "I'm here for you, how can I support…."

And then there is Carley. Well…where do I begin. You have been my right-hand woman in my businesses for eight years. You work with a great measure of talent, creativity, and loyalty. I would not be anywhere near where I am today without you. For this book, alone, you are the solo agent of graphics, marketing, and tech support. Saying, "Thank you" will never be enough.

Thank you to Chris, Kathleen and all the colleagues of Christian Counseling of South Tampa. Your belief and support of me and my clients are immeasurable.

Todd, the journey on my road to a PhD, the research and dissertation, culminating in this book began in 2010. Thank you for always believing in me.

John, well, you know. Apart from my writing coach and editor, you were the next person to read the manuscript in its entirety. Your care will be held forever in my heart.

To all my tribe, too numerous to name, thank you. You all know who you are. You have walked me through times of celebration and heart ache! Thank you for being on this journey with me.

A NOTE TO PASTORS, PRIESTS, AND MINISTRY LEADERS

Thank you for your dedication to the health and well-being of marriages—by reading this book and serving in various capacities in faith-based institutions and organizations.

It is concerning that the divorce rate is 50% even within faith communities where couples identify themselves as Christians. However, the divorce rate is significantly lower among Christian couples who actively and regularly practice their faith. I find this extremely hopeful. We are all needed—pastor, priests, ministry leaders, and therapists alike—if we are going to win the battle of seeing marriage, as designed by God, thrive!

I consider my work as a licensed Christian marriage therapist as my calling. I believe in my position in the community and partnership with local pastors, priests, and ministry leaders. I view my work as an arm of the various discipleship programs of the church, helping people grow in their faith and become the best version of themselves. I have been partnering in this capacity for well over 30 years.

I realize that as shepherds, you take your role of looking out for the flock very seriously. It is difficult to consider referrals to professionals outside of the church if you are not aware of their individual standing, their belief system, their support of the local church, their training, and how they conduct themselves professionally. Knowing this, I have designed two ways for us to get to know one another.

1. I offer a lunch webinar a few times a year. You can find more information and a registration form at: www.shanonrobertscounseling.com/partnerships. If there isn't a date close to your desire, please feel free to contact us in order for us to send you the replay.

2. I also offer a free 30-minute phone consultation. You can register for a phone consult at: www.shanonrobertscounseling.com/consultation. I would be honored to speak with you.

A NOTE TO THERAPISTS

Thank you for your work and life pursuit in attending to the emotional and mental health of your clients. Your work is so needed and extremely rewarding. Evidenced-based practice indicates that is ethically challenging and contraindicated to serve as a person's individual and couples' counselor. Consequently, I am always looking for professionals that desire to work together in a referral partnership.

I work in a format that allows couples to come to me from every part of the world, and they need a network of options to choose from as they return to their communities. In your work with individuals and/or couples of faith, it's likely that you see significant differences in the ways they view marriage.

I learned a great deal about this when I carried out my dissertation research, adding to the body of literature in this arena; now, I offer a free webinar periodically throughout the year in order to share this information. If you would like more information and/or to register, you can do so at:

www.shanonrobertscounseling.com/therapist-partnership.

If there isn't a date that works for you, please let me know and I'll send you the replay.

I also offer a free 30-minute phone consultation that will allow us to get to know one another and create a mutually beneficial partnership. I consider it an honor to speak with other like-minded professionals like you. You can register for a phone consult at: www.shanonrobertscounseling.com/consultation.

THE CULTURE OF A CHRISTIAN MARRIAGE

In my doctoral research, I investigated the nuances of how Christian couples are influenced by their cultural backgrounds in how they conduct and/or view their marriages. To download a fact sheet summarizing this research, visit: www.nakedandexposedbook.com/resources.

HOW TO WORK WITH DR. SHANON

Choosing who to work with for marriage counseling can be daunting. I have developed an eBook to help you: *How Not to Make the Biggest Mistake When Restoring Your Most Important Relationship: 6 Things to Consider When Choosing Marriage Counseling.* You can download the eBook at: www.nakedandexposedbook.com/resources.

Through recent research and many years of experience, I know that the traditional approach to couples counseling doesn't produce the positive results that therapists or clients are seeking. Many couples postpone therapy for years before they call me. Typically, when they finally do call, they're in a crisis or stuck. Hourly counseling every week or every other week doesn't provide immediate relief. In addition, many couples find it hard to work out scheduling or drop out due to disillusionment with the process. Many couples determine that counseling doesn't work or won't work for them.

When I moved to an intensive model of therapy, I began to see better results and success for my couples. Intensives allow couples to get a full round of intervention and help at the front end of therapy. The follow-up program provides necessary support and accountability for them to stay on track afterward. Additional benefits of the intensive model include the following:

- It provides couples with options for counseling outside their local communities.

- Couples can choose the professional with the most expertise or a therapist who incorporates their beliefs into the experience.
- Doing an intensive gives couples the opportunity to take time away from all the distracting stressors of life to focus on their relationship.
- Traveling to an intensive in another city can feel like counseling and a vacation at the same time.

You can find more information on my website at:
www.shanonrobertscounseling.com/mmw.

Throughout the year, I periodically offer a free webinar for couples to begin their counseling journey before committing to further intervention. It's an honor for me to serve couples in this capacity. The webinar provides information you can apply to your relationship immediately and gives you an opportunity to get to know me better. To learn more about the webinar and/or register, visit:
www.shanonrobertscounseling.com/webinar.

I also offer a free 30-minute phone consultation to anyone who wants to discuss the unique needs in their relationship. You can schedule a phone consult at:
www.shanonrobertscounseling.com/consultation.

Dr. Shanon speaks at various conferences and churches. You can check for scheduled events and/or learn more about booking Dr. Shanon to speak at your event on her website:
www.shanonrobertscounseling.com/events.

END NOTES

Chapter 1

1. All Bible verses included in this book are quoted from the Holy Bible, New International Version®, NIV®, ©1973, 1978, 1984, 2011 by Biblica, Inc.®.

2. John Gottman, *What predicts divorce?: The relationship between marital processes and marital outcomes.* Psychology Press, 2014.

Chapter 3

1. Mernitz, Sara E. "The Mental Health Implications of Emerging Adult Long-term Cohabitation." Emerging Adulthood 6, no. 5 (2018): 312-326.

2. John Bowlby, (1988). A secure base: Parent-child attachment and healthy human development. New York, NY: Basic Books.

Chapter 4

1. Tronick, Edward Z. "Things still to be done on the still-face effect." Infancy 4, no. 4 (2003): 475-482.

2. John Gottman, The Gottman Institute, https://www.gottman. com.

3. Ellie Lisitsa, "The Four Horsemen: Criticism, Contempt, Defensiveness, and Stonewalling." The Gottman Institute (Blog), April 23, 2013. https://www.gottman.com/blog/ the-four-horsemen-recognizing-criticism-contempt-defensiveness-and-stonewalling.

Chapter 6

1. Wade Rowatt, and Lee A. Kirkpatrick. "Two dimensions of attachment to God and their relation to affect, religiosity, and personality constructs." Journal for the scientific study of religion 41, no. 4 (2002) 637-651.
2. Marion Solomon, "Helping intimate partners to heal each other." Healing moments in psychotherapy (2013): 195-215.
3. Myers, Joshua. The relationship of prayer and forgiveness to God attachment, romantic attachment, and relationship satisfaction in Christian married adults: A mediation study. Liberty University, 2015.
4. Brown, Brené. *Rising Strong: The Reckoning. The Rumble. The Revolution*. Random House, 2015.

Chapter 7

1. Brené Brown. *Daring greatly: How the courage to be vulnerable transforms the way we live, love, parent, and lead*. Penguin, 2015.

ABOUT THE AUTHOR

Dr. Shanon Roberts is a licensed professional counselor, author, speaker, marriage repair expert, founder of the *Intimacy for Life Method*™ and host of the *Love Leading Podcast with Dr. Shanon.* For over 30 years, she has worked with thousands of couples helping to restore broken relationships. As the founder of Christian Counseling of South Tampa, LLC, she uniquely built a center of professional counselors partnering with local churches. She

has moved her experience and influence into creating Shanon Roberts Counseling, LLC, where she offers in-person and online programs for couples and women, free webinars, weekly live shows, and retreats. Her approach is enriched with empathy and acceptance, even while addressing the most sensitive of subject matters in session. As a Christian, she is sensitive to the spiritual part of individuals, knowing that faith and practices can be an avenue to peace and incorporates this dimension into treatment at each couple's comfort level. Her marital restoration approach offered in two-day intensives has allowed her to work with one couple at a time from all over the United States.

Dr. Roberts has spoken at marriage conferences, mother'
groups, women's retreats, recovery programs, and more. She ha.
presented her dissertation and research at the American Associ-
ation of Christian Counselors. She lives in Tampa, Florida and
when not working, enjoys spending time at the beach and with
her three grown children.

Made in the USA
Coppell, TX
18 August 2024

36176720R00094